SIR FREDERICK OUSELEY

and

ST MICHAEL'S, TENBURY

A Chapter in the History of English Church Music
and Ecclesiology

EDITED BY WATKINS SHAW

Fellow of the Royal College of Music
Honorary Librarian of St Michael's College, Tenbury, 1948-85

Published for
THE TRUSTEES OF ST MICHAEL'S COLLEGE, TENBURY
by the UNIVERSITY OF BIRMINGHAM

SIR FREDERICK OUSELEY AND ST MICHAEL'S, TENBURY

Sir Frederick Arthur Gore Ouseley in the robe of an
Oxford Doctor of Music c.1856

CONTENTS

THE OPINIONS EXPRESSED BELOW ARE PERSONAL TO THE RESPECTIVE WRITERS.
THEY DO NOT NECESSARILY REFLECT THE VIEWS OR POLICY
OF THE TRUSTEES OF THE TRUST DEEDS RELATING TO
ST MICHAEL'S COLLEGE, TENBURY

EDITORIAL PREFACE

When, under unhappy necessity, St Michael's College, Tenbury closed in 1985, some historical account of so individual an institution seemed called for. What follows is an attempt to supply this.

My first thought was to amplify and bring up to date the *History of St Michael's College, Tenbury* (London, SPCK, 1943), edited by M.F. Alderson and H.C. Colles. But I found that I wished to introduce so much additional material *in medias res* that any attempt to interpolate this in my own style into the graceful manner of the chapters contributed thereto by my old tutor H.C.C. would have produced an incongruous effect. Therefore I have tackled the subject anew, whilst incorporating Canon Alderson's recollections and the accounts of the Music Library and the buildings from the 1943 book.

In one or two directions I have slightly extended the limits of the subject beyond what is strictly relevant. Thus, although at least some account of the Founder's family background was clearly called for, I have enlarged on this somewhat because it seemed interesting in itself yet unlikely to find another forum; so also the background to his Oxford degrees in music. On the other hand, apart from his childhood compositions I have not discussed his work as a composer, editor, or writer on music. This is certainly not the appropriate place to submit that to critical appraisal.

It is desirable to comment on some matters of terminology. In choosing the title *Sir Frederick Ouseley and St Michael's, Tenbury* I am well aware that the expression 'St Michael's, Tenbury' carries no exact connotation. But it has come into common use; and although my principal subject is the College, it allows me where necessary to treat of the Church to which the College was so curiously related. Next, with regard to St Michael's Church, while it is understandable that generations of St Michael's boys should have regarded it as 'chapel', this is incorrect and wholly misinterprets the Founder's view. I have been careful to avoid the term. But I have not interfered with the use of it by Canon Alderson and Heathcote Statham because the way they and other *alumni* felt, even though wrong, is one of the facts about the College. The expression 'collegiate church', however, is much to be deplored in this connection.

The correct style of the Founder is 'Sir Frederick Ouseley'. Except in contexts of particular formality requiring the use of all Christian names ('Sir Frederick Arthur Gore Ouseley'), recognised standard usage for knights and baronets is of a *single* Christian name prefixed by 'Sir' and followed by the surname. To speak of 'Sir Frederick Gore Ouseley' therefore suggests (and has led some people to assume) that his surname was the compound 'Gore Ouseley'. This is not so. His mother was 'Lady Ouseley': had he married, he and his wife would have been 'Sir Frederick and Lady Ouseley' (not 'Sir Frederick and Lady Gore Ouseley'). True, he kept alive his relationship to his illustrious father by signing himself sometimes (but by no means invariably) 'Frederick A. Gore Ouseley', but that is a rather different matter.

In Chapter 8 I have mentioned a few members of the teaching staff by name, feeling that the service they had rendered was such that it was impossible to pass them over. I hope that others will not feel slighted thereby. I am well aware that St Michael's has been fortunate in many members of staff who have served it at less than their rightful reward. One is conscious of the debt owed to them even though they cannot all be named.

It is a disappointment not to include the late Christopher Hassall's 'Poem for Michaelmas Day'. Notwithstanding that this made its first appearance in the *St Michael's College Magazine* in the centenary year 1956 for which it was expressly written and that it was a central feature in the Appeal Brochure of 1960, the author's widow, through her agents, has felt unable to give permission for its inclusion here except on payment of a fee. In view of the foregoing circumstances, and also because all other contributions and editorial work have been willingly given without financial recompense, it did not seem appropriate to meet this charge.

ACKNOWLEDGMENTS. I acknowledge with humble gratitude the gracious permission of Her Majesty Queen Elizabeth II to quote the passage from Princess Victoria's Diary in Chapter 2. I am also grateful to the Trustees of St Michael's College, Tenbury for permission to reprint the reminiscences of M.F.Alderson (Chapter 9a) and the accounts of the Music Library and the buildings (Chapters 10 and 11) by E. H. Fellowes and Sir Charles Nicholson respectively; to the Royal School of Church Music for permission to print Heathcote Statham's reminiscences (Chapter 9b); and to the family of the Reverend John Hampton for allowing access to some of his papers.

W.S. 1986

CHAPTER 1

THE OUSELEY FAMILY

by the Editor

No fewer than six Ouseleys, spanning the years 1762 to 1889, score entries in *The Dictionary of National Biography.* In one generation there are four, namely Sir William Ouseley (1767-1842) and his brother Sir Gore Ouseley (1st baronet, 1770-1844) together with their two cousins, the brothers Gideon Ouseley (1762-1839) and Ralph Ouseley (1772-1842). Gideon was a noted Irish evangelist, and Ralph eventually became a major-general in the Portuguese army and a Portuguese knight. The succeeding generation provides Sir William (Gore) Ouseley, KCB (1797-1866) and Sir Frederick (Arthur Gore) Ouseley (2nd baronet, 1825-89), the founder of St Michael's College.

The family could boast long lineage. Tradition maintained that in the 13th century it was settled in Shropshire. And there the Ouseley of that day, recently married to one Agnes, rode out to welcome King Edward I en route to Wales. Agnes was attacked by a black wolf emerging from a holly thicket, which bit off her right hand before the gallant husband was able to kill it. To this incident is ascribed the addition to the family arms (hitherto simply *Or, a chevron and chief sable)* of three holly leaves, and a grant of the crest 'a black wolf's head erased with a right hand in its mouth couped at the wrist, gules, and a ducal coronet'. The heraldic motto then became *Mors lupi, agnis vita* (the death of the wolf [is] life to the lambs), the word *agnis* being of course a play on the name Agnes. In his manuscript volume of *Parentalia* recording this, Sir Gore Ouseley added with uncomfortable vagueness, 'An ancestor of the Ouseley family has left an account of an ancient monument in a church in Shropshire on which were the figures of the warrior and the fair Agnes, the latter represented as wanting the right hand'.' As to the holly leaves, all those familiar with St Michael's College will recall the architect's apt use of them, for example in the carved cornice of the library, and in the exterior spandrels of the hall windows.

From tradition we move to firm ground with Richard Ouseley (†1598) by whose time the family was settled at Courtenhall (now Courteenhall), Northants, where his altar tomb remains in the church. His son, Sir John Ouseley, knighted by James I, lost his life at the siege of Breda, 1624. The Courtenhall property was forfeit in the Civil War and Sir John's two grandsons eventually settled in Ireland. The line was continued in the younger of them, Jasper, whose descendant Ralph (1740–1803) was the grandfather of the founder of St Michael's College. According to his younger son's account, Ralph Ouseley was 'an eminent Antiquary and an excellent scholar. He was also skilled in numismatics and possessed a good collection of coins, celts, and other antiquities'. He is buried in St Mary's Church, Limerick. Presumably it was through him that Sir Frederick Ouseley owned the manuscript of an early Irish medical treatise, now in the National Library of Ireland.

Both his sons, who were educated privately along with Gideon Ouseley, evinced strong interest in the East. The elder, William, who was knighted by the Lord Lieutenant of Ireland, studied Persian in Paris and Leyden and began his series of significant publications as early as 1795 with *An Essay to facilitate the Reading of Persian Manuscripts.* But our interest is with the younger son, Gore.[2]

Gore Ouseley (there seems no explanation for the choice of Christian name) went out to India in 1787 to engage, at first, in commerce. In his leisure time (to quote his own words in a letter to his father) he studied

> Persian, Bengalese, and Hindu, and a little Arabic and Sanskrit. I also read over a good many classics, that an education so liberally given, may not be thrown away by neglect. In music and drawing I am much improved, – the former is my favourite study. A-propos, I feel more disappointed than I can tell you about the bagpipes. I was sanguine in my expectations of their arriving this year.[3]

But presently at Lucknow he came to be of valuable service to the British power through friendship with the nabob vizier of Oudh. Thus he attracted the very favourable notice of Marquess Wellesley, the Governor-General, whose Indian Despatches (afterwards printed) contain high commendation of Gore Ouseley. On this account, after his return to England in 1805 he was created a baronet.

In 1806 he married Harriot [sic] Georgina Whitelocke. Lady Ouseley's ancestry might, if anything, prove more interesting than her husband's. Her father, John Whitelocke (1757-1833), having attained the rank of lieutenant-general, was sent in command of a force to recover Buenos Ayres in 1807. The attempt failed and on account of his misjudgment he returned to be court-martialled and cashiered in 1808. He himself was of modest parentage, his father being agent to the Earl of Aylesbury. But *The Dictionary of National Biography* remarks that he was 'probably a descendant of Bulstrode Whitelocke' (1605-75), thrice a Commissioner of the Great Seal under the Commonwealth and Protectorate and a celebrated Ambassador to Queen Christina of Sweden. The secure genealogical link has not been established, but it has been stated, presumably on the strength of Sir Frederick Ouseley's own understanding of the matter, that Lady Ouseley's father was a great-grandson of Sir Bulstrode Whitelocke.[4] (The knighthood, by the way, though Swedish, was recognised in England.) Furthermore, it seems significant that in Sir Frederick's possession there survived a manuscript, presumably inherited from his mother, in Bulstrode Whitelocke's hand. This document[5] begins:

> The 24 day of October 1655 my noble and kind friend Doctor Thomas Winston dyed att his lodgings in Gresham Colledge London...And by his last will & testament...he gave all his lands in Essex to my sonne Bulstrode...

and then deals at length with the protracted proceedings arising from the very problematical circumstances of this will.

Another apparent link which, while somewhat uncertain, is too strongly suggestive to be brushed on one side is the fact that Sir Frederick Ouseley owned a magnificent Bible and Prayer Book which he kept apart from his main library and which both contain the bookplate of his grandfather, John Whitelocke. Both books have matching bindings embroidered in silver bullion-work on light-blue velvet depicting the Stuart coat-of-arms with the cypher of King Charles II, 'C II R'. The arms are also shown on the fore-edge paintings. John Whitelocke himself was not a collector of books, and it is therefore impossible to resist the thought that his possession of these testifies to a family relationship to the 17th-century statesman and ambassador. In 1919 they were bought by H. M. Queen Mary (consort of George V) and are now among the most striking of the finely-bound books in the Royal Library at Windsor Castle. For further consideration of these books, see Appendix A below.

In 1810 Wellesley, now Foreign Secretary, selected Gore Ouseley for an important mission to Persia (Iran) in the high rank of Ambassador-extraordinary and Plenipotentiary. The significance of the mission lay in Napoleon's ambitions to reach India, a goal to which Persia was an avenue. It was therefore more than desirable to discourage any rapprochement between France and the Shah and to secure a treaty of friendship between England and Persia. This was the more so because at the time France and Russia were in alliance, so that Russia, on bad terms with Persia, was not indisposed to exert pro-French pressure on her. In July 1810 Sir Gore, accompanied by Lady Ouseley and their three-year-old daughter Mary Jane ('Janie', who was later to play her part in Frederick Ouseley's earliest musical efforts), set off for the Persian Gulf via Bombay. Proceeding thence to Teheran, he used his opportunities to enjoy the antiquarian treasures en route and indeed acquired some sculptures and inscriptions from the palace at Persepolis which he presented to the British Museum. After many curious incidents he succeeded in concluding the Treaty of Teheran in 1812, whereupon the Shah conferred on him the Star of the Order of the Lion and Sun 'adorned with resplendent jewels to be worn on the breast'[5] and the right to display two armed Persian warriors as supporters to his coat-of-arms.[6] He also presented him with a gold plate, heavily enamelled and showing the lion and sun in the centre (see Appendix B below), and in addition he wrote to the Prince Regent recommending that the Ambassador should be raised in rank.

At this point Russia became detached from her alliance with Napoleon and entered into treaty with England. Gore Ouseley thereupon devoted his efforts to a rapprochement between Russia and Persia (Treaty of Gulistân, 1813) and in consequence was invited to St Petersburgh to receive the thanks of the Czar. In Russia he was everywhere received, as he himself expressed it, *en prince*. He was given the insignia of the Order of St Alexander of Newsky in diamonds and the Czar's portrait set around with the same jewels on a snuff box. Furthermore the Emperor told him he had the Prince Regent's promise to raise him to the peerage.

Already before leaving Persia a son and heir had been born to the Ouseleys, named Wellesley after the Foreign Secretary and Abbas after the Crown Prince of Persia. Now in Russia the family was further enlarged by a another daughter. She was baptised in the Winter Palace with the Emperor (by proxy) and the Empress (in person) among her sponsors; furthermore, as Sir Gore with pardonable pride recorded in Lady Ouseley's Bible, 'the child was held at the font by the Empress'. For these reasons the little girl was named Alexandrine.[7]

After his return to England following an absence of just over five years he was not asked to undertake any further public duty, nor apparently did he seek any, but retired into private life with a pension of £2,000 a year. After his somewhat heady experience in Russia he may well have been disappointed not to receive a peerage. However, he was sworn of the Privy Council in 1820 following the accession of George IV, and in 1831 he was appointed Knight Grand Cross of the Royal Guelphic Order by William IV. It may perhaps be significant that this was conferred by the monarch in his capacity as King of Hanover, and so did not require the recommendation of the British Prime Minister.

At first, apart from his London residence, he lived at Woolmer's, a house near Hertingfordbury, Herts (which gave its name to a hymn tune composed by Frederick Ouseley), and then at Hall Barn near Beaconsfield. Pursuing his intellectual interests, he was elected a Fellow of the Royal Society in 1817 and likewise of the Society of Antiquaries in 1818. The bookplates in very large numbers of the books in his library display his armorial bearings after the grant of the Persian supporters, and therefore relate to the years of retirement. He played the violin and improved his musical skill by a course of instruction from J. B. Logier,[8] a noted pedagogue of the day who also gave lessons to the Misses Ouseley. Probably he also played the viola, for he owned a fine Amati instrument dated 1620.[9] As a committee member he was active in promoting the Royal Academy of Music and on the establishment of that institution in 1822 became one of its directors. He was a prime mover in setting up the Oriental Translation Fund Committee of which he was chairman and under whose auspices his *Biographical Notes on Persian Poets* was posthumously published. He was also President of the Society for Publication of Oriental Texts. He clearly devoted much of his spare time to the construction of genealogical tables tracing his descent not only from numerous noble families, but from Kings of England and France, not to speak of Charlemagne or of more exotic figures such as *El Cid*. These he wrote out himself in several albums decorated by heraldry of his own painting.[10] We are told that he also exercised his skill in ivory turning, a craft acquired in the east.[11]

His retirement was saddened by the death of his heir, Wellesley Abbas, at the age of 10 in 1824, but there was compensation for this in the birth during the following year of another son, Frederick Arthur Gore, to whom we shall turn in the next chapter. Gore Ouseley died on 11 November 1844 and was buried in Hertingfordbury Church where there is a memorial to him.[12]

To round off this family account it may be added that as the male line of both Sir Gore and Sir William Ouseley failed after the first and second generation respectively, any male descendants of Ralph Ouseley, their father, must be sought through their half-brother Joseph Walker Jasper

Ouseley, his son by a second marriage. A collection of 35 oriental MSS which had belonged to Gore Ouseley was sold by his son to the Bodleian Library, Oxford, and according to the *Summary Catalogue*, vol 4, p. 664, it appears probable that other oriental MSS of Sir Gore were later sold or presented by Sir Frederick to the Bodleian. It was from Ouseley MS 140 there that Edward Fitzgerald became acquainted with the *Rubáiyát* of Omar Kayyám in 1856.

CHAPTER 2

FREDERICK OUSELEY: THE EARLY YEARS, 1825-50

by the Editor

The home and family into which Ouseley was born on 12 August 1825 was thus one of assured social standing, financial independence, leisure, and culture, proud of a long lineage and also conscious of having done the state some service. Much of this was reflected at his baptism on 16 May 1826 by his uncle, the Revd William Spencer Whitelocke, when he was named after personages no less than H.R.H. the Duke of York (Frederick), the great Duke of Wellington (Arthur), besides his father (Gore), and when the sponsors present included the Dukes of York and Wellington as well as the Marchioness of Salisbury. A more homely touch was the inclusion of his sister, Mary Jane.[1]

He was evidently a pretty child. In 1832 the Duchess of Hamilton gushingly wrote, 'The little fellow's countenance is a noble one - very delicate, with full dark eyes, and a very prominent and expansive forehead.'[2] This is well borne out by two portraits of him as a child. The first, a tinted pencil sketch of head and shoulders by H.B.Ziegler, *c*1835, emphasises the delicacy of countenance beneath fair hair. The second, a charming full-length portrait in oils done by John Lucas in his characteristic large-scale manner shows the boy seated at a piano.[3] It reveals a winningly attractive face with broad forehead beneath wavy hair. As the Benjamin of the family with an elder sister more than 17 years older, he may well have been petted by the womenfolk.

His fine sensitivity to musical pitch and his mental grasp of harmony was noticed at a very early age. When only four, for instance, he could correctly observe of a piece of music played by a band in Brighton that it was 'a kind of F, but neither F natural nor F sharp'. His father, mother, and elder sister could all understand this unusual talent, and Mary Jane in particular had the technical competence to enter into, and discuss with him, his precocious interest in harmonic progressions and modulation.[4] As such a child will, he soon began to make up little pieces at the piano, and both his mother and sister had the musical literacy to write these down before he was old enough to do so himself. Many of these transcripts Ouseley himself preserved with his musical library to the end of his life.[5] The earliest of them goes back to 1828. A programmatic piece made up when he was six years and seven months old depicts the progress of an illness he had experienced. It is naive harmonically, but he is not afraid of a tonal adventure into C flat minor, and he explores the range of the keyboard with confidence.[6] In 1832 he improvised a simple little dramatic piece, *Tom and his Mama*. Next year, more ambitiously, he set Metastasio's libretto *L'isola disabitata*. This has its interest as showing early talent and resource, but to say, as even so competent a judge as William Ayrton did (if correctly reported by Miss Ouseley), that Haydn's setting of that text was much inferior to it, is to be absurdly obsequious.

Beyond the domestic circle, two of his early pieces, a March in C and an Air in A flat, achieved wider notice by being printed in an anthology, *Original Compositions...to which is added, some Vocal and Instrumental Music*, published by Lloyd of Harley Street in 1833 'for the benefit of a family in reduced circumstances'. The March was given further circulation by its reproduction in *The Harmonicon* for 1833. It is something slightly more than a miniature of simple harmonic outline and regular figuration. It shows resource of sonority, bars 19-24 are quite imaginative, and there is a bold feeling for tonal colour in bars 17-18. These features must be accepted as authentic, even though the piece may have been touched up a little when committed to paper by his mother or sister, for it will be noticed that some of the chords require a hand span not likely in a child of six (see the end of this chapter).

Describing this as 'one of the most marvellous productions of this age of musical wonders', *The Harmonicon* goes on to give the following account of the boy 'on the authority of a gentleman, in whose report we place the most implicit confidence':

> He has received no instructions in music, and though taught by himself to play with considerable skill on the pianoforte, does not know his notes on paper, and trusts to his sisters for writing down what he composes. He improvises entire scenes, singing to his own accompaniment, the latter often exhibiting harmony the most recherchée, chords that an experienced musician only uses with caution; but these are always introduced and resolved in a strictly regular manner, not by rule, for he has learnt no rules, but by the aid of a very surprising ear, and of some faculty, which, for want of a better term, we will call intuition. His organ of hearing is so fine, that, with his eyes closed, he instantly names any musical sound produced; and so discriminating is this sense in the child, that, when a note is struck on an instrument, tuned either above or below the usual pitch, he immediately discovers and accurately states in what the deviation consists. A chord of four notes being sounded, he named each note exactly, though at some distance from the instrument, and with his back turned to it.[7]

But he is referred to in a more illustrious source even than *The Harmonicon*. In 1836 three Persian princes called on the Princess (later Queen) Victoria at Kensington Palace, and the services of Sir Gore were enlisted to accompany them, together with Lady Ouseley. Something must have been said on that occasion about the boy, for on the next day, 14 July, the Princess wrote in her journal:

> At 2 came Sir Gore, Lady, and Miss Ouseley with their little 'Musical Prodigy', Sir Gore and Lady Ouseley's son, called Frederic [*sic*], only 10 years old. This boy is really the most wonderful child I ever saw; he plays and sings beautifully, and composes songs, whole operas, etc. without knowing a note of music.[8]

One wonders whether some imperfect version of this incident lies behind the statement that 'at some period or another in his youth, Frederick Ouseley is said to have played duets with H. M. Queen Victoria at Buckingham Palace'. In some reminiscences immediately following Ouseley's death, a former (unidentified) organist of St Michael's College remarked that he had heard him say that he played a duet on the pianoforte with Mendelssohn at six years of age when the composer was visiting the family.[9]

Before leaving the subject of his early compositions, one must mention a curiosity, remarkable in view of his subsequent direction, published by Novello in 1834: a duet,

Vanne a regnar ben mio, Duetto per Soprano e Contralto Composto e Dedicato alle Honbles Emma & Catherine Maynard da Frederick Arthur Gore Ouseley all' età di otto anni. Extending to 106 bars, this displays familiarity with operatic duet style and vocal *fiorature* in a way that might have filtered through from Donizetti.

It may be thought that a child of these distinctive gifts would have been considered destined for a career in music and have had his education directed accordingly. Not so, however, at that time for anyone of Ouseley's background. However much Sir Gore might help to promote professional musical training through the Royal Academy of Music, it would be unthinkable to him that his son - the heir to a baronetcy - should adopt music as a career. Consequently these gifts were never conditioned by, or exercised in, the main stream of English musical activity, be it as composer, conductor, teacher, or man of affairs, like Henry Bishop, William Sterndale Bennett, Cipriani Potter, or Arthur Sullivan, not to mention Charles Hallé and Michael Costa, or another notable amateur of music, George Grove, all of whom were at work in his lifetime. Thus his musical proclivities were to be directed into a different channel entirely.

There is nothing to suggest that Ouseley ever received any disciplined training in music whatever, and he evidently had to rely purely on his own observation and reading coupled with natural endowment. As for general education, like his father before him he did not go to school. Already by the age of six he was learning French from his governess and Latin from a tutor.[10] In his teens he was sent to be educated privately under the Vicar of Dorking, James Joyce.[11] The Vicar's son, James Wayland Joyce, some 13 years older than Ouseley, was at that time his father's curate. He and Ouseley became firm friends and, as we shall see, Joyce's influence on the younger man was important. He then went up to Christ Church, Oxford, as an undergraduate with the rank (as a baronet's son) of Gentleman Commoner in 1843. At what stage he made up his mind to be ordained we do not know, but it is more than likely that under the influence of the younger Joyce his thoughts already by then tended in that direction. This may not, however, have been his father's intention, for in a sermon preached at the Jubilee of St Michael's College in 1906 the Revd T. A. Ayscough said that 'in his father's mind he had been destined for quite another calling'.[12] However, his two sisters were certainly inclined to High Church piety.

To anyone in Oxford, especially if thinking of Holy Orders, these were exciting times, dominated by the immediate controversies of the Tractarian, or Oxford Movement. Only two years before Ouseley went up, the Heads of Houses had condemned Tract XC (incidentally, Ouseley owned a complete set of these Tracts), and in 1842 Newman had resigned the living of St Mary's, the University Church. In 1843 Pusey, though a Canon of Christ Church and Professor of Hebrew, was suspended from preaching before the University, and February 1845 saw the wild scene in the Sheldonian Theatre when W. G. Ward was deprived of his degrees. Later that year Newman seceded to Rome. At the heart of all this turmoil there were anxious questions occupying the minds of many thoughtful men about the Church of England as a spiritual society free from Erastianism, and these problems made their impression on Ouseley.

Another trend of ecclesiastical thought in the 1840s, though less celebrated than that of the authors of the *Tracts for the Times*, cannot have failed to impress Ouseley. This resulted from the work of John Jebb (1805-86), who in 1843 became Rector of the village of Peterstow in Herefordshire. The main thrust of his argument was that the services of *The Book of Common Prayer* were by their nature and in their essence intended to be sung, and that the choir, assisting the clergy in this, ought to be seated in the chancel with them. Because of his appeal to history this accorded with the romantic strand in the texture of Tractarianism and so tended to become identified with it. Nevertheless, it was quite independent, and indeed of no concern to the original Tractarian leaders themselves. Those familiar with Hardy's *Under the Greenwood Tree* will smile at Jebb's assertion that to place a church choir in the west gallery is 'popish', and there are many today who deplore the acceptance of his influence in certain conditions. Yet influential his ideas were indeed to prove, much assisted later on, it should be said, by Ouseley's work.

Jebb's own contribution was serious and learned, based on much original investigation. He first unfolded his ideas in lectures delivered in Leeds in 1841, published as *Three Lectures on the Cathedral Service of the Church of England*, and they were to some extent instrumental in arousing in certain Leeds parishioners a wish for a daily choral service (and it will be recalled that before the end of that year S. S. Wesley had been invited to become organist of Leeds Parish Church). Jebb's more fully developed argument was put forth in *The Choral Service of the United Church of England and Ireland* (1843), followed in the year after Ouseley left Oxford by the first volume (1847) of his valuable *The Choral Responses and Litanies of the United Church of England and Ireland*, of which the second volume appeared ten years later.

Not, however, that in the midst of all this Ouseley's undergraduate life was unduly serious. F. W. Joyce recounts stories of his practical jokes and happy nature, also hints that he may not have over-applied himself to study. Music played a considerable part. He organised concerts, got up glee-singing on the hall staircase of Christ Church, and in his last year acted for some months as organist of the Cathedral in the interregnum between the departure of William Marshall and the arrival of C. W. Corfe.

Ouseley was still an undergraduate when his father died, whereupon, a few months after his 19th birthday, he inherited the title and became 'Sir Frederick Ouseley'. There are suggestions that Sir Gore's death affected his son's performance in his Oxford finals, in which it had been expected that he would distinguish himself in mathematics.[13] As it was, his attainment at the end of 1845 was anything but distinguished. In those days candidates for honours were examined in two disciplines, classics and the elements of mathematics and physics. The names of those in the first four classes were printed, while only the number of those in the fifth class was indicated. Ouseley obtained a fourth class in maths and physics, but in classics he was among the unnamed of his year in the fifth class.[14]

Having fulfilled residence for his BA degree in April 1846 he settled down to study for ordination and lived mainly with his mother and sisters in London, singing in the choir of their recently-established parish church, St Paul's, Knightsbridge, where the outlook accorded with that of the Tractarians with the further attraction of a choral service. But he also paid long visits to J. W. Joyce, now Rector of Burford (3rd portion), Salop. Burford lies on the river Teme where the boundary of Shropshire marches with that of Worcestershire at Tenbury Wells, so it was on these visits that Ouseley first came to know the part of the country where he was later to establish his church and college.

While working for ordination he must also have been training himself in preparation for the Oxford degree of B Mus which required him to submit an original work for choir and orchestra displaying competence in the craft of composition, including of course counterpoint and fugue. Such a degree was an odd goal for a young baronet of independent means, and there is an anecdote to the effect that Dean Gaisford tried to dissuade him from what was thought unbecoming in a gentleman. The status of the degree was wholly anomalous. No residence in Oxford was necessary, for indeed the University provided no course of instruction. All that a candidate had to do, without any preliminary examination, was to prevail on some college to allow him to place his name on the books for a short time and, when thus registered, to submit his 'exercise' to the approval of the Professor of Music who himself was not required to live or teach in Oxford. Indeed, until 1855 no Oxford Professor of Music was a full member of the University as an MA. After approval, the exercise had to be publicly performed in

Oxford, a discouraging factor which put the candidate to the considerable expense of engaging performers. Neither the Bachelor's nor the Doctor's degree in music was much sought after. At Oxford there were only 35 such graduations in the 50 years 1800-49, none of them relating to Oxford men in any true sense. That Ouseley should have wished to take a degree of this kind can perhaps be supposed to rest on his desire to link his musical gifts with his service in Holy Orders and, with that in view, being an amateur, to proclaim his competence in the world of music.

He took his ordination examination in 1849 when, offsetting his showing at Oxford, he headed the list of candidates.[15] He was made deacon on 3 June and, as it happened, on the very next day Sir Henry Bishop, as Professor of Music, wrote to indicate his approval of Ouseley's exercise for the B Mus degree, a cantata *The Lord is the true God*. After expressing 'considerable pleasure' and saying that 'your concluding Fugue, in particular, does you great credit', Bishop supplies a fairly extensive list of detailed amendments, subject to which he agrees to issue the necessary certificate.[16] Coming from the composer of *Home, sweet home* and *Lo, hear the gentle lark*, these are of sufficient interest to merit some account in Appendix C below. The regulation public performance of the exercise duly took place, and in 1850 the University was treated to the unusual spectacle of a reverend baronet (a Master of Arts to boot) proceeding to the (then) lowly B Mus degree.

As a newly-fledged deacon Ouseley served as honorary curate in his own parish of St Paul's, Knightsbridge. It was a parish of some significant characteristics. To the north its parish church and highly prosperous residential part lay close to Hyde Park. To the south it stretched to the river to take in the poor area of Pimlico. The Vicar, W. J. E. Bennett (1804-86), combined profound allegiance to Tractarian principles and belief in choral services with intense pastoral concern, and he realised that his poorer parishioners could never be adequately reached or served by the fashionable parish church. Accordingly he raised funds to build a daughter church, St Barnabas', Pimlico, within the parish.[17] And not only a church. There was a parish school for 600 pupils and, built on to the church, residential accommodation in which he and his assistant curates lived a common life as a notional 'St Barnabas College'. There was also provision for twelve chorister boys, trained, educated, and clothed free, living in the 'College'. Both Morning and Evening Prayer were rendered chorally each day. Ouseley presented the organ, and he also contributed generously towards the cost of the choir.

When he began in June 1849 the new church was not ready. But services were held in the school and he took up residence in the College, there to make enduring friendships with two fellow curates, G. F. de Gex and Henry Fyffe. It was a sphere of work which seemed very appropriate for him. Nonetheless trouble was not long in coming. Even before the church was consecrated he wrote to his friend Joyce on 23 January 1850, 'We are full of trouble here', and ended by pleading 'Pray write - I am in terrible depression of spirits on this account'.[18] It appears that Bennett and some associates had obtained the opinion of 'counsel learned in the law' and been advised that a decision of the Privy Council on a matter of doctrine would be binding on them in virtue of the ordination oaths of supremacy and allegiance. This advice was deeply disturbing to them. The background to this was the case of *Gorham v. the Bishop of Exeter* which had been referred to the Judicial Committee of the Council. Mr Gorham, it will be recalled, had been refused institution on account of what the Bishop considered unsound views on Baptismal Regeneration. That Bennett and his friends (who included Manning, Pusey, and Keble) should be considering their position before judgment was delivered shows how scrupulous they were. It was not so much what the judgment might be (though in the end it was for Gorham and so, in effect, against them) as that a doctrine of the Church should be pronounced upon at all by an arm of the State under the Royal Supremacy.[19]

This was quite intolerable to Bennett. If he could not hold a doctrine pronounced by an authority he could not accept, should he not retire into lay communion? On the same grounds Ouseley began to feel that for his part he should move to the Scottish or American Episcopal Church. In an immensely long, closely reasoned letter,[20] Joyce (who, of course, would have agreed with Bennett as to doctrine) sought to reassure Ouseley on the ground (broadly speaking) that an oath need not be taken *ex animo imponentis* (i.e., in the sense of the person proposing the oath), but in the sense of what the person making the oath thought the proposer meant. This is a fine distinction indeed to exercise the mind. Bennett was unconvinced, and Ouseley remained perplexed. So the matter hung in the air; and though no decisive action immediately ensued on Bennett's part it was unsettling enough before a further problem arose.

Late in September Ouseley wrote 'in great perplexity' to Joyce as follows:

> I must, according to the invariable and tyrannical rule of my Bishop, take Priest's Orders at Christmas. But I cannot and will not consent to do so at St Barnabas, as it is only my being in Deacon's Orders which saves me, as you know, from doing many things sorely against my conscience. It is therefore essential to get away; but I am loth to do so without something definite to go to - not a curacy, because of the scandal it would give against Mr Bennett, who has enemies enough ready to take hold of any pretext to defame him. Bennett himself is quite willing I should go at Christmas; and I am also quite sure it is necessary both for my health and happiness to do so.[21]

What things were against his conscience are not known, but they must have related to some feature in the Communion Service which he had not been personally responsible for while only a deacon. However, only six weeks after the date of that letter more dramatic events were encountered. The style of observance at St Barnabas' had begun to incite a 'no-Popery' rabble, and on the evening of Saturday, 9 November Ouseley, as he recounted in a letter to his old Oxford friend John Rich,[22] was insulted and threatened in the street. The next day there were rumblings in the morning and it was thought prudent to cancel the evening service at St Barnabas'. Ouseley, however, preached at St Paul's in the evening and on returning to the College overheard groups of men threatening what would happen next Sunday. This gave some forewarning against the uproarious disturbance which occurred inside the church on 17 November, but even so it required 100 policemen outside to keep the mob in check. On the following three Sundays there were equally, if not still more, disgraceful scenes for, in addition to intruders within, in Bennett's words 'the crowd outside the church was battering the doors and threatening to break in, the police resisting'.[23]

While all this was going on, Ouseley, following his letter of September, was considering his next step and appears to have thought of taking a parish himself. But on 22 November he wrote to Joyce announcing that he had abandoned this idea for the present. 'I must go abroad for a year, at least. My health requires it, *and many other motives incline me to it'* (present writer's italics).[24] Accordingly, by the end of 1850 he severed his connection with St Barnabas' and the parish of St Paul's.

As it happened, Bennett, because he could not be disloyal to his Bishop, resigned at the same time.[25] The effect was that the personnel of St Barnabas College now dispersed. Both de Gex and Fyffe left, and the future of the twelve boy choristers hung in the balance. That was the catalyst for St Michael's College.

0 † 0 † 0 † 0

NOTE. As Ouseley was to be pursued by a certain amount of suspicion at Tenbury on account of his former association with the ritual at St Barnabas', the opportunity is taken to set out here exactly what this embraced (the term 'ritual' being somewhat broadly interpreted).

1. Altar cloths coloured according to the season.
2. Eastward position of celebrant at Holy Communion.
3. Two lighted candles on the altar at Holy Communion.
4. Choir communicated before the congregation.
5. Surplice worn for preaching, and Invocation and Sign of the Cross used before the sermon.

6. Choir and clergy entered and left the chancel in procession, the clergy making a reverence to the altar.
7. Ringing of bells before services.

It is not quite clear whether wafer bread was used. A proposed revival of vestments was not put into effect. Daily choral Morning and Evening Prayer was held to be 'ritualistic'.[26]

MARCH

Composed at the age of six

Frederick A. G. Ouseley

Some obvious engraver's errors in the text of *The Harmonicon* (1833) have been silently corrected.

CHAPTER 3

THE FOUNDATION OF St MICHAEL'S CHURCH AND COLLEGE

by the Editor

On the breaking up of the little community in Pimlico Ouseley was conscious of the undischarged obligation to the boys in the choir of St Barnabas' and made himself responsible for it. Accommodation was secured at Lovehill House, near Langley, Bucks (to the west of the present M25, between M4 and M40). Thither the boys were taken to be educated, provided for, and to go on singing under the charge of Henry Fyffe.[1] Some loose memoranda[2] in an unknown hand covering the years 1851 to 1858 which came to light in 1964 show that nine boys (six choristers and three probationers) were at Langley to start with. Of the full Pimlico complement of twelve, some may perhaps have been due to leave and some may not have wished to go. By September 1856 when St Michael's Church was consecrated, none of the nine was still a choir boy, but two of them took part: A. J. Capel as an alto and J. C. Büdinger as a tenor. Both continued as lay clerks of St Michael's. Capel, his way perhaps smoothed by Ouseley, graduated at Trinity College, Dublin, became an assistant master of St Michael's College, ordained, and eventually a minor canon of Hereford Cathedral, while Büdinger took charge of the parish school at St Michael's. More significantly, these memoranda name as 'lay clerk' and 'assistant master' John Hampton, later to be Warden of St Michael's. He was already over 15 years old when St Barnabas' School was ready, but earlier he had been a chorister at St Paul's Church, where he recalled Bennett's catechism class, as we know from his own account.[3] He went on to be associated with St Barnabas', and so came to accompany Fyffe and the boys to Lovehill House.

How far Ouseley's thoughts at this time looked further ahead than simply honouring an obligation to a particular little group of boys we do not know. Perhaps at first he had nothing more in mind. Be that as it may, when his thoughts developed this small nucleus was to hand for their purpose.

These arrangements made, he set off for Lisbon in company of de Gex. From Portugal he travelled through Spain and Gibraltar to Rome and Venice, visiting churches, trying organs, examining antiquities (getting up Livy, Pliny, Tacitus for the purpose in Rome), but disliking Italian church choirs and becoming confirmed in antipathy to the Church of Rome.[4] In Rome he got to know the organist of St Peter's, the director of the Sistine Choir, and the renowned collector, the Abbate Fortunato Santini. In a letter to Joyce in May 1851 he wrote:

> By means of these three worthies I have been able to make very extensive and valuable additions to my own private collection of classical musick, already not a contemptible one. So that I hope ere long to be spoken of – *monstrari digito praetereuntium* – as the possessor of a most enviable musical MS library.

Some of the things he derived from Santini (none spectacular) can be identified in Ouseley's library; one, now Tenbury MS 623, has a Latin dedication to him in Santini's writing.

From Italy, via Switzerland, he went on to Germany where at both Dresden and Leipzig he was immensely struck by the singing of the boys. 'I am quite certain I shall never care for English Cathedral trebles again', he wrote at the end of October. 'You never in your life heard anything approaching it...I suspect they are chosen from a somewhat higher class of Society than our own choristers usually are'.

All the while his miscellaneous thoughts for the future were gradually becoming clearer and drawn together. Things are best told by means of extracts from his letters to Joyce:

> 9 May 1851. With regard to a living...my final plans must be *in nubibus.* Much depends on events which are coming on the Church: much depends on my health, which is very indifferent just now: much, too, depends on a sort of offer I have had of a precentorship at Winchester...Still, in spite of all this, I may, after all, settle down into a country parson. If so, I had rather be near you. You see, I have scruples about hiding my light under a bushel. I think I clearly ought, if it be possible, to devote it to God's service in His Holy Church. Now in a regular country living this is impossible: for a large town living I have neither health nor strength. A precentorship is more the thing: but it has its

drawbacks and they are of no small weight. So, on the whole, I am pulled all ways...

1 September 1851. I really must not delay any longer sending you a letter...to speak a little of the Ludlow affair in which you have so very kindly interested yourself. I have determined to undertake it...But there are difficulties still. *In primis,* I cannot afford to build the Church and endow it too. My income will not do it, and I cannot touch my capital...What I have in my thoughts is a Church in the 14th Century style, with Collegiate buildings adjoining, for residences for myself, two Curates and Choir, and Cloisters, too, enclosing a private portion of the Cemetery. Now, this plan is expensive, and so I can only accomplish it by degrees. I will give £1,000 every year towards this building, if anyone else will help me in any degree proportionately...Then as to the Service. I must have a daily choral Service: my choir must be a model choir.

26 September 1851. I think I like the Ludlow scheme more and more. The only difficulty I foresee is money. You see, my funds are rather reduced now in consequence of all I disbursed at St Barnabas both toward the Church and Choir...I will not do without daily choral Service. I have no talent for teaching, no powers of preaching, and no health for hard parochial work. But God has given me one talent; and that I am determined to devote to His Service, and offer it up to adorn His Church.

21 October 1851. Fyffe requires my assistance at his place on Christmas Day, and I have promised to go and look after my protégés there, which is of course a duty as well as a pleasure.

28 October 1851...it is very desirable indeed to raise the position of our English Choir boys. Now they are too often mere rabble...Now, my choral scheme will tend...to improve this state of things. I hope also that by instituting a model choir I may supply another great deficiency, i.e. choir men, brought up as Choristers, who shall know how to be reverent and devout in Church...But yet further, as some chorister boys will become professional musicians, so others may wish to be ordained. Now there is a great lack of good chaunting clergy in the Church of England. No man can be so fit to perform the Priest's part well, in a Choral Service, as he who has been brought up as a Chorister boy.

Short of drawing up a systematic memorandum of intention, Ouseley could hardly have made things clearer than by these passages. To begin with, whether or not the precentorship of Winchester was actually offered him, he appears to have considered, and rejected, the idea of that sort of work. On the face of things it seems to us something that might have fitted him admirably. Moreover, one can hardly think that anyone in his position could not have had such a post if he so desired. The conclusion must be that pastoral parochial work was a considered choice. But the parish had to fulfil certain conditions - not a large town parish, for which he felt ill-equipped, and not a 'regular' country parish. His service to the Church must be through his musical gifts. He must be able to have daily choral services. It seems to follow, then, that to obtain these conditions he must procure the allocation of a parochial district and build a church himself. To provide for the daily choral services he must have a choir, and so, with the experience at Pimlico behind him, he proposed a sort of college for this purpose. And had he not the nucleus of a choir waiting in the wings at Lovehill House? Further, the college might prove an instrument of wider usefulness than simply supplying a choir for his parish church. It might give a better education than was generally available for choir boys; it might help to provide future generations of devout choir men; and it might improve the supply of 'chaunting clergy'. Finally, he proclaimed the intention that his choir must be 'a model choir'.

There was one other supplementary impulse of a very different character, not mentioned in these letters. Ouseley felt that in founding a church and college he was making a certain restitution. In his little book *The Doom of Sacrilege* (London, 1886), J. W. Joyce wrote (p.119) that one of his own friends

> supposing that aforetime some temporal advantage had accrued to his patrimony from a sacrilegious source, has at the sacrifice of a large portion of that patrimony far exceeding any tainted accretions, built and founded a College, which he moreover now maintains, for training up Ions, skilful in the more elaborate services of God's temple, and for giving them such an education as may fit them for His ministering servants on earth hereafter.

To whom could this conceivably apply but to Ouseley?

After his return from the continent nothing more is heard about his problem of conscience concerning Church and

State. Not that it is likely his views changed. But as to what he called 'the National Church' or 'the Church of these Realms' he had his own work to do, and kept apart from further controversy in which Bennett and others continued to be involved; and after some initial suspicion, his own conduct in later years at Tenbury aroused no hostile reaction on grounds of ritualistic practice.

Why and when the 'Ludlow' scheme fell through we do not know. It is said that Ouseley also considered a site in the Oxford diocese but was not welcomed by Bishop Wilberforce, whose two brothers, once associates of W. J. E. Bennett, had seceded to Rome; and that there was even a possibility that he might have restored and built upon the ruins of Buildwas Abbey, Salop.[5] But in June 1852 Ouseley bought some land in the area of Old Wood, on the outskirts of Tenbury where his Church and College were later to rise. 'June!', wrote H. C. Colles,[6]

> Who would not buy land [adjoining the Old Wood Common] who saw it in June? Its pastures, its springing crops, its orchards when the fruit is firmly set; its prospects...all call to the traveller to stay. Would he have been less precipitate if he had had to make his decision in January?...the disadvantages of this spot as a centre of education leap to the eye more readily in winter...problems of transport, catering, and particularly those of the domestic and medical care of small boys; difficulties of finding lay clerks...of employing and keeping them when found; these and a thousand other considerations were not likely to be present to Sir Frederick's mind, as he drove between rose-clad hedges...

The purchase may have been a shade premature, for there was no assurance that any parochial district could be assigned in the neighbourhood. Indeed, the Vicar of Tenbury, John Churton, out of whose parish some part of the district would probably have to come, was actively ill-disposed towards Ouseley by reason of his late connection with St Barnabas', Pimlico. For a little time, therefore, Ouseley wondered whether he should establish simply his College with its own chapel in the hope that a parish might be formed later.[7]

But at this juncture a wholly independent factor came into play and helped him to proceed. The leading family of J. W. Joyce's parish of Burford was that of Rushout: George Rushout (heir-presumptive to, and subsequently holder of, the barony of Northwick), and his unmarried sisters Harriet and Georgina, living at Burford House, now the site of a well-known nursery garden. George Rushout was lord of the manor of Tenbury, and it appears they had been conscious of some need for a church in the remoter part of Tenbury which now interested Ouseley. In her will, made as early as May 1849, Miss Harriet Rushout had allotted £600 'towards the erection of a church on the Old Wood in the Parish of Tenbury'.[8] Although Ouseley must have met the Rushouts on his visits to Joyce, he apparently knew nothing of this idea (had Joyce any inkling?) until it was disclosed on her death in August 1852. Seizing the unexpected opening, he set about attaching his scheme to this. He was helped not only, of course, by Joyce but also by the good will of William Norris of Tenbury. Mr Norris, a solicitor, was the first of five successive partners in the firm of Norris and Miles who have gone beyond what mere duty required in guiding the affairs of St Michael's College throughout its existence.

Above all, the way was smoothed by the courtly good offices of two clergymen of the neighbourhood, the brothers Thomas and John Miller. Thomas was the squire of Bockleton and patron of the living of that village as well as that of nearby-by Leysters. John Miller, who acted as assistant curate in both parishes and with whom Ouseley conducted his correspondence, did not himself completely approve of his ideas, as we shall see. Nevertheless, recognising their sincerity and generosity, he set out to help and to allay local suspicion. In spite of Churton, the Bishop of Hereford (who himself had no reason to love Tractarians) approved, a parish district was formed out of Tenbury, Leysters, and Middleton-on-the-Hill, building was begun, and on 3 May 1854 the foundation stone of the new church of St Michael was ceremonially laid by James Wayland Joyce.[9]

While all this was going on, Ouseley's headquarters were with Fyffe and the others at Lovehill House, where a stable loft was fitted up as a chapel. The small community there was not static. It had become something more than a mere safety net for the ex-St Barnabas boys. As others joined and the originals fell out, it adopted a rudimentary organisation into 'choristers', 'probationers', and 'commoners'. Ouseley was regarded as Warden, Fyffe as Headmaster and Fellow, and R. W. Norman (who took over from Fyffe as Headmaster when the move to Tenbury was made) first as Fellow, then as 'Honorary' Fellow. So by now there was an informal embryo college.[10] John Hampton remembered those days:[11]

> While at Langley we were well employed in keeping up the grand Cathedral use besides concert work in madrigal and other secular music. Sometimes we had a man from Windsor as in Wesley's *Wilderness*. We were badly off for Basses. [Hampton himself was a tenor.] At times we had visitors such as Sir John Goss, Dr [E. G.] Monk, Dr Corfe, Mr G. Cooper, and then we attempted big things, such as *Israel in Egypt* and *Messiah*.

For Ouseley's larger intentions the years 1852 and 1853 were a time of waiting and planning. He took the opportunity to put forth the fruits of some of his own musical endeavours in the shape of two publications, the first an anthology of his own *Cathedral Music* (Novello, 1853) comprising five services and seventeen short anthems, the second *A Collection of Cathedral Services by English Masters of the 17th and 18th Centuries* (also Novello, 1853). Although the first included the favourite *How goodly are thy tents*, its general standard, according to Sir John Stainer, furnished grounds for criticism when, a few years later, Ouseley was appointed Professor of Music at Oxford.[12]

The next two years, 1854 and 1855, saw Ouseley's accession to three dignities. By 1854 he was ready to submit his exercise for the degree of D Mus, an oratorio of sub-Mendelssohn character entitled *The Martyrdom of St Polycarp*. This time Sir Henry Bishop had no reservations. On 5 September he wrote that he had 'no hesitation in giving it my unqualified approval. Indeed, it does you infinite credit.'[13] When the work received its statutory performance on 9 December in the Sheldonian Theatre ('with unprecedented completeness and effect', as an unidentified newspaper cutting has it) the composer was able to engage forces of first-rate calibre. The band was led by the highly experienced Henry Blagrove; the vocal soloists were among the best of the day: W. H. Weiss (bass), W. H. Cummings (tenor), and Charlotte [Sainton-]Dolby (whom Mendelssohn later had in mind when writing the contralto solos in *Elijah*); the trio, 'In the sight of the unwise', which kept the name of Ouseley's oratorio alive after its other pages had faded, was sung by boys from the Chapel Royal. Among this galaxy John Hampton was entrusted with a minor solo part.[14] Ouseley proceeded to his doctorate on 18 December 1854.

On 1 March 1855 the Bishop of Hereford wrote to invite him to become Precentor of his Cathedral.[15] After explaining that the Ecclesiastical Commission had appropriated the revenues of the post so that, in his phrase, *stat nominis umbra*, the Bishop went on to say that he thought it important that it should be preserved and 'worthily embodied in some living Person'. Bishop Hampden has been criticised[16] for his attitude in this, but it seems to me very fitting. Despite the Commissioners, he did not want this office to be disregarded and, on the prospect of having Ouseley in his diocese, he used the opportunity to welcome him by an altogether appropriate compliment.

Ouseley was not involved in regular or frequent attendance at Hereford, and his strictly obligatory duty was limited to preaching on Christmas Day. Hereford is a cathedral 'of the Old Foundation'; thus Ouseley ranked next in dignity to the Dean in Choir, and yet had no voice or vote in Chapter. In constitutional theory, however, the control of the Cathedral's music lay in his power. The day to day work was in the hands of the succentor, but he showed interest and exerted influence when he could, for example in the re-building of the organ in 1862, in composing his Complete Service in C and the anthem *Blessed be Thou* (both for double choir) for the re-opening of the Cathedral in June 1863, and in the appointment of Langdon Colborne as organist in 1877. There is an anecdote - how reliable, who can say? - that he used his constitutional control of the Cathedral's music to compel an unwilling dean to hold an early morning celebration on some important day simply by a threat not to allow any music later in the day. It was not until he joined the Chapter on appointment as canon in 1886 that Ouseley was drawn more closely and regularly into contact with the Cathedral's affairs.

Then, on 30 April 1855, Sir Henry Bishop died. Without looking further afield or more ado, the Oxford proctors, in whose unfettered hands this small appointment lay, announced on 8 May that they had chosen Ouseley to succeed him as Professor of Music.[17] Lest present day conditions should mislead, let it be said that this was no outrageous plurality, incompatible with his main work at Tenbury, and that it commanded only a modest stipend of £100 a year. There was no department of music in any modern sense, no staff of lecturers, no curriculum or teaching. In one way the post was rather like the professorship of poetry, except that it was held for life, not a term of years. Its duties were simply to examine for music degrees and to give occasional lectures of general interest to a public audience. Ouseley improved matters by instituting examinations (one of them, following the example of Dublin and Cambridge, in general subjects) in addition to the exercise, and he brought in other examiners to be associated with him. But no undergraduate instruction in music was given until after his time, and residence was still not required for degrees in music. Nevertheless, his reforms, modest as they were and conditioned by lack of resources, were the very first steps towards the proper establishment of music within the Oxford academic structure. Moreover, he was faithful in giving public lectures which, though generally venturing only into shallow waters, helped to promote cultivated interest in music in Oxford generally, while his own personal status helped to improve that of music. Gradually, more candidates came forward for the degrees, including one or two who had taken an arts degree.

Finally, while work was going forward on the site of St Michael's Church and College, Ouseley at last proceeded to the priesthood, being so ordained in Hereford Cathedral on Trinity Sunday 1855. In rather more than a year's time, with the Church but not the College completed, the moment arrived to bring his boys from Lovehill House to temporary accommodation at Spring Grove, a house at the other end of Old Wood Common, Tenbury, in readiness for the consecration of the new church.

An account of that occasion must form the start of a new chapter. Here we may round off the more mundane part of the tale. On top of the cost of the ground on which the Church stands and of the small college estate, Ouseley's building accounts as finally settled in 1858 amounted to £22,011: Church, £7,047; College, £13,713; unapportioned additional costs, £1,251. In the immediate ensuing years there were further costs of £500.[18] These figures (rounded to the nearest £) take no account of the cost of the large 4-manual organ which was also paid for by Ouseley. And to the tally of his generosity must be added the endowment of the living of St Michael's parish which at first amounted to £60 per annum but which was quoted in *Crockford* in the year of his death as worth £200. Miss Rushout's £600 was probably subsumed in all these costs, and there were other generous contributions: Miss Georgina Rushout partly paid for the fine east window glass (by Hardman), while Sir William Cope (like Ouseley, a musical baronet in Holy Orders) bore the cost of the masonry of the west window.[19] Nevertheless, Ouseley's personal munificence was without stint and burdened him for a few more years with a mortgage of £1,500 on the security of the College property and an additional one on the security of private valuables.

From the time of its consecration in 1856 St Michael's Church passed into the hands of the appropriate ecclesiastical authorities. As for the College, it was as yet without endowment. Its running expenses, far in excess of the very small fees which came in, were borne by Ouseley from year to year. Looking ahead, in 1858 he drew up a paper[20] which survives in an envelope endorsed in his hand: Memorandum / St Michael's College / Its Prospects / What it wants / 1858

The paper reads as follows:

To pay off the mortgage on the College	£1,500
To pay the remainder of Bills incurred in fitting it up	500
To build a Tower and west cloister	3,000
To endow the Wardenship	5,000
Headmastership	2,500
Six choristers	4,000
Organist	1,500
Three [lay] clerks	4,000
Fabric funds	1,000
Total	£23,000

> The first and most important object is to get the College clear of mortgage - it could then be conveyed to Trustees and be endowed. The gentlemen recommended to be Trustees are 1. Col. Rushout, 2. Revd J. W. Joyce, 3. Revd J. J. Miller, with power to add to their number to the number of five in all & to be bound to supply vacancies as they occur. The perpetual advowson of the Perpetual Curacy of St Michael's shall be made over to these Trustees - & this with intent that when the living falls vacant, they may nominate to it such a clergyman as will be best qualified and willing to keep up the daily choral services in St Michael's Church as now conducted.
>
> The next most important object for which aid is solicited is the endowment of the different offices in St Michael's Coll. in the order in which they are set down in the above list. Thus, and thus only, can this College be rendered independent and perpetual.
>
> I commend these objects to those whom God has blessed with the means and heart to do good to such Church schemes. May He inspire them with such a love for the improvement of the choral service of our Church & the spiritual advancement of those who are to be trained here to serve it, as may induce them to help forward this good work, for Christ's sake in Whose Holy Name it has been undertaken.
>
> Frederick Arthur Gore Ouseley, Warden of St Michael's

Even this scheme, it may be added, stopped short of mentioning the stipend of the choirmaster and the reduction in fees to probationers.

But, whether from diffidence, or some active discouragement, or any other reason, no such appeal was prosecuted. And here we have one of the fundamental weaknesses of Ouseley's College. Its funding continued to rest entirely on himself and the institution had no broad base of public support. This contrasted markedly with the earlier and contemporary work of Nathaniel Woodard, who established his schools (aiming at a different purpose) by successful fund raising and with the support of influential public figures. Whether Ouseley's aims could have achieved the response which Woodard achieved may be doubted. Yet without something of the kind its permanence was likely to be in question, as Ouseley recognised.

In January 1864, immediately after discharging the mortgage, he did convey the College land, buildings, and contents together with a tiny endowment (mainly in the form of rents) to trustees, as also the advowson of St Michael's parish with the provision that they should appoint the Warden of the College to the living. The Trust Deed promulgated a body of Statutes which declared that

> The object of the College is...to form a model for the Choral Service of the Church in these realms ... [and] for the furtherance of this object to receive, educate, and train boys in such religious, musical, and secular knowledge as shall be most conducive thereto.

The Statutes also gave formal recognition to Ouseley's conception of a body of Fellows to whom was allotted the election of future Wardens.

So at least a continuing legal entity was created. Yet in practice nothing was changed and the Founder continued to supply an annual subvention. A stray Bursar's Cash Book[21] survives covering the period 1878-84 and, selecting at random the College years 1880-81 and 1881-2, we find it reveals the following figures (to the nearest £):

		1880-81	1881-2
Annual expenditure		£3,379	£3,499
Endowment income:	Dividends	29	29
	Rents	325	363
Ouseley's contribution		1,600	1,350

Thus the Founder's own contribution plus the yield from endowment created by him accounted for half the expenditure. And in assessing these figures it has to be borne in mind that the College enjoyed its 'plant' free of charge and was not called upon to pay a Warden's stipend. As a matter of interest, in those years the annual salaries of the three principal assistants (all resident, of course) were: Organist (Claxton), £150; Headmaster (Sayers), £130; Choirmaster (Hampton), £120.

As parson of the parish Ouseley felt a further obligation was his - the provision of a parish day school. The building which served for this until its closure in 1937 lies across the road from the College lodge and is now known as Cadmore Close. It was not built until 1870 and there is no Log Book earlier than 1875. But there can be little doubt that he arranged for such a school in some sort of accommodation almost from the start. In his own hand in his Register of the College, against the name of J. C. Büdinger as lay clerk, Spring Term 1858, he wrote 'Parish Schoolmaster', and in one of his early letters to Miller he refers to George Rushout's desire that there should be a church day school in the parish. As curate, John Hampton raised funds by voluntary subscriptions for the building, to which one has little doubt Ouseley contributed. According to Mr A. S. Miles he took the entire management of the school and made himself responsible for the expenses, the annual income being raised by voluntary contributions, by far the largest coming from himself.[22] Büdinger remained as schoolmaster until his death in January 1889.

In 1870 occurred also the last development of the 'plant' of the parish when, with the aid of a grant from the Ecclesiastical Commission, Ouseley provided a vicarage (subsequently occupied by Wardens Hampton and Swann) close to, but outside, the College grounds.[23]

Against this background one can the more readily appreciate a reminiscence of C. W. James (Commoner, January 1871 to August 1872) who wrote:[24]

> [Ouseley] was wrapping himself in an old blue cloak and stepping into a farmer's shabby little gig to be driven to Tenbury station, en route to Oxford or Hereford. Suddenly he turned to me and said gently, 'You know, I was not born to drive to stations in one

> of my own tenant's gigs, nor to wear the same cloak which I had at Christ Church as an undergraduate'.

The constitutional arrangements of his Church and College were unusual and make it hard to provide a succinct answer to enquiries asking 'What is St Michael's, Tenbury?' There being no convenient term, no wonder there has been misunderstanding. Nevertheless, Ouseley's friend Rich should have known better than to describe it as a 'collegiate church'[25] - hence the use of the term in M.F.Alderson's reminiscences in Chapter 9 below. It would have saved much legal and administrative difficulty had it been so. (A collegiate church is one established for and administered by a self-governing group of clergy - usually dean and canons - acting in a corporate capacity with a common seal, so forming a college in the strictest sense.) St Michael's Church, however, is and always has been simply a parish church with the usual churchwardens and an incumbent licensed by the diocesan bishop. Instead of placing his College in the hands and under the governance of the Church, as presumably he might well have done, Ouseley chose to give it separate existence by the Deed of 1864. But, as patrons of the living, the Trustees of that Deed were bidden to present the Warden of the College as incumbent provided he was qualified. Church and College, each a distinct entity in law, were formally linked only by this provision. Of all misconceptions, however, none is so gross as that of Sir Nikolaus Pevsner (*Worcestershire* [The Buildings of England], 1968) who with all his prestige designates the Church as 'R.C.'

CHAPTER 4

The First Sixty Years. 1856-1916

by the Editor

In the presence of between six and seven hundred people, St Michael's Church was consecrated on Monday, 29 September 1856 by Renn Dickson Hampden, Lord Bishop of Hereford, who preached at the Choral Matins immediately following the ceremony. Then, at an ensuing Communion Service (not choral), more than three hundred people received the Sacrament. Later in the day there was Choral Evensong when Jebb significantly chose to preach on 'The Principles of Ritualism Defended'.[1] A large choir was assembled. Ouseley's own ten boys were augmented by four other trebles, one of them, A. J. Caldicott from Worcester, later to become a minor composer, another, Arthur Sullivan of the Chapel Royal, destined to a fame which needs no mention. There were 31 men, 16 of whom (including the Founder) were clergymen. The four altos, of whom he was one, were outnumbered by 12 tenors and 15 basses. Among the visiting singers were James Wayland Joyce, John Jebb, the Master of the Children of the Chapel Royal (Helmore), Sir William Cope, and Drs C. W. Corfe and E. G. Monk, organists respectively of Christ Church, Oxford, and of York Minster. The organ was played by (Sir) George Elvey of St George's Chapel, Windsor, and Sir Frederick Ouseley himself, now Vicar (strictly, Perpetual Curate) of the parish, intoned. For both morning and evening he chose Benjamin Rogers's Service in D, an evident favourite of his. That for such an occasion he should have selected something which seems to us now drably nondescript is a striking instance of changed taste. The anthems were, in the morning, Boyce's *I have surely built thee an house*, and in the evening, Goss's *Praise the Lord, O my soul* (composed for the Festival of the Sons of the Clergy, 1854), and Elvey's *O praise the Lord of heaven*, specially written for the occasion. In Goss's anthem, Sullivan was the treble soloist. Ouseley did not thrust himself forward as composer on this occasion, confining himself in that capacity to his hymn tune *Woolmer's* which was written for it.[2] The event

> caused the greatest interest for many miles around. Every lodging in Tenbury and its neighbourhood was engaged. The roads were lined with carriages...so that only a limited number of those who came could gain admission to the church itself.[3]

After this resounding beginning there was a lull. The College buildings were not yet complete. Against the boys' names in his Register for the Michaelmas Term Ouseley wrote 'mainly absent', so it was not until February 1857 that the sequence of daily choral services at last began. Meanwhile, feeling that some public recognition of Ouseley's action should be made, John Miller had been collecting subscriptions from residents in the local Rural Deanery, that of Burford. Writing in March 1857 to present Ouseley with £272 to furnish a stained glass west window, Miller referred to his 'disinterested munificence and piety' and his 'noble work'. But with this letter he sent a private note, for two purposes. First, to let Ouseley know that one person approached had written to say that 'not knowing whether St Michael's is intended to carry out the ceremonial practices and principles of St Barnabas, Pimlico, I am unwilling, by subscribing, to give countenance to anything of that kind'; and second, to make a personal explanation. He wrote that he must honestly confess himself

> largely dissentient from what I cannot but think the hyper-ritualism of St Michael's; and also, that the whole scale of the establishment is something altogether different from what we had any conception of here, when the subject of a site was first broached. Hence it has been a main object with ourselves throughout (I speak as if my brother was not lost) to conciliate just forbearance towards what is unquestionably a startling innovation in these parts, and obviously open to unkind constructions. And it seemed desirable to show, by holding out the right hand of fellowship, that your work was not regarded with fear or jealousy by persons of such old-fashioned pattern and notions as ourselves; nor yet by the Bishop, or by any officials of the Deanery. But we have all along regarded the extent of your plan as a great local mistake; and I would fain express an earnest hope that you will be careful not

> to damage a good cause by any such form of excess as might possibly lead to unthinking resistance...

In reply to the official letter, Ouseley expressed thanks for the good will thus shown towards St Michael's Church, and referred to 'my endeavours to do something to promote God's glory and the salvation of souls in this place'. In answer to the private note he wrote:

> I suppose then that the quantity of music in my weekday & Sunday evening services is the point to which you take exception. I therefore make no apology for telling you the reasons which have induced me to start a full choral service - only I must first premise that for fear that such a service should be offensive to any of my flock, I have two common parochial services every Sunday, whereof the 2nd at 3 p.m. is totally devoid of all music whatsoever, & the 1st at 11 a.m. is only diversified by two Psalm tunes congregationally sung.[4]

The rest of this well-expressed, rather moving letter will be found in Appendix D below. That was on 14 March 1857. However, reference to the Register of Service Music,[5] which begins to run from 8 February 1857, shows that on nine Sundays between Easter and 28 June 1857 there was in fact Choral Matins. Presumably, then, this was in addition to the 'two common parochial services'. But thereafter the Register strictly reflects Ouseley's letter inasmuch as, with the rarest exceptions, there was no music on Sundays throughout his life except at Evensong.

But on Sunday evenings and six weekday mornings and evenings, with only two choir vacations a year, there was music in plenty. From the outset the advantage of having boys already trained at Lovehill House was evident, so that a copious repertory could be drawn on straight away, without any need to build it up gradually. With 13 choral services weekly and a College year of 40 weeks, there were upwards of 16,500 choral services during the 32 years of Ouseley's wardenship. In view of his declared emphasis on such daily services, and his wish (in the words of the 1864 Statutes) 'to form a model' for such, then the prime interest of his foundation, particularly under his personal regime, must lie in its church music. But in order not to interrupt such flow as this narrative may possess, consideration of it is reserved for separate discussion in Chapter 5.

When he used the word 'model' one has little doubt that Ouseley was looking for something additional to musical quality pure and simple, and that he had in mind the whole manner in which the services were conducted and the attitude and deportment of those taking part. As to musical achievement we have only the solitary testimony of Sir John Stainer, who said that 'choral services of a high standard of excellence were maintained':[6] and that is the opinion of a distinguished authority. For this the credit must go almost wholly to John Hampton, who held the key post of Choirmaster throughout Ouseley's time, and later continued to hold it when he succeeded to the wardenship. No doubt it was a great benefit to him to work with boys under residential conditions on the spot, as compared with the system of day boys which many cathedrals operated. For men's voices there were always three, sometimes four, lay clerks. Judging by the music used, one has no doubt that both Ouseley (alto) and Hampton (tenor) also sang with the choir, and it appears that the choice of Headmaster and any assistant was conditioned by what they could contribute to the choir.[7] Additionally, fitful assistance was given by a few adults called 'Commoners' or 'Students of music' who came to the College to read and study and to imbibe its ethos generally.

On the face of it this would provide a good body of men, sometimes up to as many as a nominal ten, but in point of fact the maximum potential was never realised. Büdinger, the tenor lay clerk, was seldom present at both daily services, perhaps because of his parish school duties. The attendance register shows that with the exception of C. F. Fox Chawner (referred to in Chapter 5), who played his part faithfully for a number of terms, the 'Commoners' and 'Students of music' contributed very little indeed, some of them practically nothing, so that, taking into account other absences, the number of men singing was not infrequently minimal. Comparison of attendances with the music actually sung on certain days shows that when 8-part music was in question (for example, Walmisley's Evening Service in B flat for double choir, sometimes used on Sunday evenings), there were only just enough voices (sometimes not even that) to cover requirements.[8]

The adult personnel of the College was completed by a maximum of 24 non-resident (and, of course, unremunerated) Fellows, of whom eight, headed by J. W. Joyce, were named at the outset. As shown by the complete list of those whom Ouseley himself appointed (see Appendix E below), these were overwhelmingly clerical, mainly close personal friends or associates, some of them former masters at St Michael's, with only a very few laymen. Though his erstwhile Pimlico colleague and helper at Lovehill House, Henry Fyffe, was included, his other close Pimlico associate, G. F. de Gex, was not, though he sent his son to the College, and that son was to become a Fellow under Warden Hampton. And while the first organist, J. C. Hanbury, became a Fellow (by that time in Holy Orders) under Ouseley, Stainer, who became organist of St Paul's Cathedral in 1872, had to wait for nomination (by Hampton) in 1894 even though meanwhile the list was not full.

What the Founder had in mind in creating such a body is not clear. It seems he hoped the Fellows would contribute by their presence to the annual Michaelmas festivities ('Commemoration'), and he committed to them (along with the so-called 'Resident Fellows', i.e., the Choirmaster and Headmaster) the responsibility of electing his successor as Warden. But he certainly did not use them in any advisory capacity, and there is no sign that such influence as they possessed was harnessed in the interests of the College. Perhaps it was an agreeable way of complimenting his friends and making a return for kindness shown. Perhaps, too, it gratified him, from the point of view of the status of his College, to complete the tally of its members by a body with the dignified style of Fellows. Mr Hampton's nominations, though less closely personal to himself, followed broadly the same pattern. But after the establishment in the 1920s of a Governing Body, two-thirds of whose members were to be Fellows, it became desirable to look for people of a somewhat different type (not always easy to find. be it said, in relation to the curious location and character of St Michael's), while future appointments ceased to be for life. These changes, however, were slow to make themselves felt.

The daily life of the College was no doubt simple and orderly, quietly and faithfully sustaining its chief purpose in the daily *Opus Dei* in church. But every year at Michaelmastide it sprang into festivity with more elaborate services, visiting preachers, and gatherings of Old Boys and visitors in 'Commemoration' of the consecration of the church.

These celebrations were at that time far more extended than under the changed social and other conditions of life in the mid-20th century. Apparently plenty of visitors were able to spare the time and find accommodation in which to stay. 'The College was filled with guests, and every available bed in the parish was taken.'[9] The occasion was spread over several days, with two principal days, one at the beginning, the other at the end. One of these provided the opportunity for a rare choral celebration of Holy Communion. Whether invariably or not, an instrumental ensemble was frequently found from College resources and visitors to accompany an anthem, players being accommodated on a platform behind the north choir stalls.[10] (Does this mean in the baptistery?) Surviving printed details for 1884 and 1885, summarised as follows, are no doubt representative.

1884

Monday, 29 Sept. 11 a.m. Matins & Holy Communion - Smart in F; Anthem: *Unto which of the angels* (Handel); Preacher (at short notice): Sir Frederick Ouseley. 6 p.m. Evensong - Smart in F; Anthem: *Lift up thine eyes* (Goss).

Tuesday and Wednesday, 30 Sept. and 1 Oct., Choral Matins and Evensong of standard character

Thursday, 2 Oct. (Commemoration Day). 8 a.m. Holy Communion. 11.30 a.m. Matins - Garrett in D; Anthem: *O praise the Lord of heaven* (Elvey); Preacher: Archdeacon Hessey; Anthem after the sermon: *To thee, O Lord* (Mozart). 6 p.m. Evensong - Garrett in D; Anthem: *Blessed be thou* (Ouseley); Preacher: Prebendary Bather.

1885

Tuesday, 29 Sept. (Commemoration Day). 8 a.m. Holy Communion. 11.30 a.m. Matins - Smart in F; Anthem: *O praise the Lord of heaven* (Goss); Preacher: the Revd G. Cosby White. 6 p.m. Evensong - Smart in F; Anthem: *Ascribe ye greatness* (Ouseley); Preacher, the Revd W. Bright, Canon of Christ Church.

Wednesday, Thursday, Friday, Saturday, 30 Sept., 1, 2, and 3 Oct., Choral Matins and Evensong of standard character.

Sunday, 4 Oct. 11 a.m. Matins, Litany, & Holy Communion - Ouseley in A; Preacher: (un-named); 6 p.m. Evensong - Ouseley in A; Anthem, *O praise the Lord of heaven* (Elvey); Anthem before the sermon: *Unto which of the angels* (Handel); Preacher, the Revd F. W. Joyce (an Old Boy).

On the evening of the day specifically designated as 'Commemoration Day', on top of all the church music, sermons, and (doubtless) gastronomic festivity as well, there was a secular concert, performers and audience somehow crammed into the small College hall. Where the music of the services was fairly predictable, that for these secular concerts offers some interesting features. In 1884, for instance, a small orchestra comprised 15 strings, two flutes, a clarinet, and a bassoon, together with (I suppose for filling-in purposes) a harmonium, played by Sayers, the Headmaster. The strings, led by Sir George Elvey, included Ouseley himself on the cello, Büdinger, the lay clerk (also cello), and his son on the violin. The remainder were presumably visitors or local players. The pianist was a well-wisher of the College from London, A. H. D. Prendergast (afterwards a Fellow). There were various glees, partsongs, and madrigals, some solo songs and instrumental items. But there were bigger pieces too, in the form of Schubert's *Unfinished Symphony* and Cherubini's overture to *The Water Carrier*, as well as a brief scene from Spohr's opera *Jessonda*. Hampton conducted. Two years earlier a fairly similar band (without Elvey, but with Walter Parratt among the violas) tackled Nicolai's overture to *The Merry Wives of Windsor* and Cherubini's to *Der portugiesische Gasthof* in a programme (again conducted by Hampton) which embraced Mozart's Clarinet Quintet, Hummel's Pianoforte Quintet,

Op.87, Pepusch's solo cantata *Alexis*, and Mendelssohn's elaborate double chorus from *Ædipus at Colonos*. How many of us today, I wonder, have heard these pieces by Cherubini and Mendelssohn? A performance of Pepusch's cantata at the present time would probably have a small fuss made of it.''

Turning now to the purely school side of the establishment, this remained small throughout the Founder's life. In all, some 240 boys were admitted before his death (an arithmetical average of 7½ a year), of whom quite a number stayed for only two years or less - sometimes very much less.[12] In each term the numbers were fairly steady from about 1860 at something like eight choristers and eight probationers with boarders touching a maximum of 17 but not infrequently falling to eight or below, and in his final term reaching only four. There was a time when he seemed anxious about numbers of pupils. Writing to J. B. Dykes on another matter on 11 February 1875 he took the opportunity to say:

> I am glad to tell you that I have now got a really good & efficient Head Master [Cooper] and that the prospects of St Michael's College are fair. After all the anxieties of last year, it is indeed a comfort to feel secure again. I wonder whether you can recommend boys to be sent here - I want to be full again & *I ought to be*... I will enclose a Prospectus in case you have an opportunity of shewing it.[13]

There were two full-time teachers, one called grandly 'Headmaster', the first being invariably, the second frequently, in Holy Orders. C. W. James, who was at St Michael's 1871-2, wrote:

> Perhaps St Michael's as a school might have prospered more than it did in its Founder's day had the masters' claims as good scholars and teachers been made the first consideration. Some of them were inexperienced, but they were certainly good men in the choir.[14]

The following table of Ouseley's Headmasters, all graduates in Holy Orders, shows that at times there was no long tenure of office.[15]

*R. W. Norman (1857)	*V. K. Cooper (1875-6)
T. Heartley (1857-62)	*H. C. Rogers (1876-9)
*F. M. Millard (1862-9)	Henry Sayers (1880-84)
*M. C. F. Morris (1869-74)	E. S. B. Fletcher (1885-8)
Henry Edwards (1874-5)	C. W. Hunt (1888-9)

Those marked by an asterisk were subsequently named as Fellows by Ouseley, and M. C. F. Morris became a trustee of the Trust set up under his will. Henry Sayers (afterwards Headmaster of Christ Church Choir School, Oxford) was the father of the writer Dorothy L. Sayers. The two full-time masters were supplemented by a visiting master for French (for many years a M. de Vit) and the College organist taught what was described as 'Instrumental Music'. A good idea of the curriculum of those days for boys of 8 - 14 years of age can be obtained from a list of 'Books in use at St Michael's College' from the Prospectus which Ouseley sent to Dykes in 1875:[16]

Bible and Prayer Book	Colenso's Arithmetic
Public Schools' Primer	Colenso's Algebra, Part I
Wordsworth's Greek Grammar	Euclid
Henry's First Latin Book	
Arnold's Latin Prose Composition, I	Smith's Smaller History of England
Arnold's First Greek Book	Douglas' Geography
Valpy's Latin Delectus	
Wilkins' Greek Delectus	De Fivas' French Grammar
Smith's Principia Latina, II	De la Voye's French Dictionary

The fees at that time were £120 a year (£60 for sons of clergy, who had preference, *ceteris paribus*, for election as probationers), £40 for probationers, nothing for choristers. 'Choristers and Probationers are taught Vocal and Instrumental Music gratuitously'. There were two vacations a year, seven weeks at Midsummer, five after Christmas. It was announced that 'the Pupils are prepared for the upper Forms of Public Schools, &c.' Fortunately education at St Michael's was not entirely encompassed by textbooks and the schoolroom alone. H.C.Lahee, who was at the College 1864-70, recalled ample opportunity to develop an interest in nature study, and dated his love of lierature from opportunities to read in the library. He wrote:

> I read all Sir Walter Scott's novels, all of Dickens, some Thackeray ... some books on travel, also Charles Reade, Wilkie Collins, and other works of repute; all this before I was 14 years of age. Most of the boys were buried in books at every possible moment that was free from school and outdoor games ... We were all keen nature lovers. In our holiday and Sunday walks we learned the habits and haunts of animals and birds ... Each boy had a collection of birds' eggs.

> We were always careful to leave some eggs for the mother bird. [17]

What kinds of parents sent boys to St Michael's? Unfortunately, of the 240 or so boys admitted under Ouseley, the father's occupation of only 107, less than half, is known. But, as one expects from the concessions and preference extended to sons of the clergy, there was a good number of boys of clerical parentage among these - 78. Fourteen fathers were service officers, six were in some form of professional work - civil engineer, medicine, etc. - one was a peer, and eight were musicians. De Gex showed confidence in Ouseley by sending his son Alexander; J. W. Joyce sent his three sons, if only for a brief period; a distant Ouseley cousin sent her son for a short time; and the musicians who sent their boys included A. J. Caldicott, George Cooper (sub-organist of St Paul's Cathedral), C. W. Corfe, Thomas Helmore (in spite of his enthusiasm for, and Ouseley's dislike of, plainsong), William Pole (FRS and D Mus), and William Spark (organist of Leeds Town Hall).

The subsequent careers of Ouseley's boys are also incompletely recorded, though we know just about half - 124 to be exact. Of these, forty took Holy Orders, and some of them became minor canons or equivalent. One can only hope - as indeed Ouseley had a right to expect - that the others carried into their parishes some of his ideals of choral worship. The Army and Navy accounted for 26, and 33 went into some form of professional work - teaching (six), accountancy, the law, banking, engineering, colonial service. A further nine are described as going in for 'business' or farming. Three more exalted ones became a J.P. and High Sheriff, Member of Parliament, or succeeded to his father's baronetcy. Of those recorded, 13 became musicians. What is interesting here is that by no means all of those had been choristers or probationers. F. W. Davenport, for example, later of the Royal Academy of Music (some of whose elementary textbooks can just be recalled by some of the same generation as the present editor), was simply a fee-paying boarder. Boys of Ouseley's era whose subsequent careers made some mark are C. J. Corfe, Charles Harriss, K.

Babington Macaulay, Charles Plummer, and G. R. Sinclair. Corfe, after service as chaplain R.N., was consecrated to be the pioneer missionary bishop of Korea. Harriss, a musician. emigrated to Canada and by marriage became possessed of means enabling him to organise (and personally conduct) huge massed choirs on imperial occasions (the latest being the Wembley Exhibition of 1924) and so to receive the Lambeth degree of D Mus. Macaulay achieved success as a solo vocalist. Plummer, a clergyman of the old school who never proceeded beyond the diaconate, was Ford's Lecturer at Oxford and the author of some respectable historical works including a once-standard life of Alfred the Great. Sinclair became organist of Hereford Cathedral and an intimate of Edward Elgar, his initials standing at the head of no. xi of the 'Enigma' Variations.

Small glimpses of some aspects of life in the College at this time have been provided by Stainer and Hampton. Of his own days as organist at St Michael's (1857-9) the former said:

> The life in St Michael's seemed, at first, primitive and mediæval. All of us had meals in the large dining-hall, Sir Frederick Ouseley and his staff occupying seats at a high table, the boys in the body of the hall. After morning service the boys settled down to their school-work, in the afternoon they came to me for lessons on the pianoforte. After evening service and a meal in hall, I studied, or practised, or, as was frequently the case, was invited by Sir Frederick to pass the evening with him.[18]

Stainer also tells how he was called upon to play through to Ouseley some of the Italian masses in manuscript contained in his library. These were written in now obsolete clefs, and Stainer records how he 'gained much from this almost unique chance of studying the vocal writers from, say, 1550-1700'. Ouseley, he remarks,

> was a capital player on the guitar, and also on the obsolete harp-lute, and often used to pass the evening singing Italian or Spanish national songs to his own accompaniment, always with admirable skill and good taste.

Hampton gives some indication of extra-curricular musical activity:

> At St Michael's we formed a pretty fair band: three cellos, two violas, six violins, clarinet, flute, and two brass, all boys or other members of the College. Once a week some 10 or 12 people from the parish joined to practise instrumental music.[19]

Writing thus in his old age, Hampton gives the no doubt unintentional impression that this combination of instruments remained uniform. What he cites is presumably a general idea of the sort of forces usually available. Probably these provided the nucleus for the little band which played at Commemoration, as already described. And at one period, certainly in 1883, at a different time of year there was an 'Annual Concert given by members of St Michael's College Choir'. In the year in question the programme began with Handel's overture to *Esther* and included a March by Claxton, the College organist of the time, described as 'Originally written for the St Michael's Boys' Band'.[20]

Of Ouseley personally there is little more to be said. He continued to navigate his barque by the compass setting determined in early manhood. If anything, he became strengthened in his emphasis on a choral form of worship. Preaching in St Peter's, Derby in December 1860 he asked 'those who have been blessed by God with voices, and ears, and musical susceptibility' to 'devote their whole powers to the praise of God', and he went so far as to suggest that the unmusical should pray for musical enlightenment and meanwhile support choral services by monetary offerings![21] Addressing the Church Congress at Brighton in October 1874 he welcomed the great progress he had observed in parish churches, but urged 'Why should not *every* parish join in the movement? Why should not every chancel be filled with devout and earnest [he neglected to say 'capable'] singers...men and boys arrayed in white robes?[22]

In January 1886 he was appointed by Bishop Atlay to a canonry in Hereford Cathedral, necessitating absence from Tenbury for the periodical months of residence. That was the only piece of preferment he ever received. He is not singular among devoted ornaments of the Church of England in obtaining little or no recognition. And yet it is hard to see what else he could have been given that would not have involved severance from St Michael's. Be that as it may, it was peculiarly fitting, if only accidental, that as Canon he should succeed John Jebb, whose ideas he had done so much to demonstrate in practical form. But we are told that, on account of the expense of rebuilding his 'ruinous' canonical house, he reaped little, if any, pecuniary benefit from the appointment. It appears that to the end of his time he had to use lodgings in Hereford when 'in residence'.[23]

One aspect of his work, usually passed over, should not be forgotten: his faithfulness as pastor of his parishioners, in the main a humble flock. One tribute at the time of his death said 'No parish in the diocese of Hereford was better cared for than this, both by himself and his earnest and helpful curate...John Hampton'.[24] This is supported in Joyce's words:

> ..he was the last man to forget that, as vicar of a country parish, he held the charge of the souls therein. The parish was worked and visited on a settled system, he himself taking one side and...the Rev. J. Hampton taking the other. Any parishioner in sickness, or in trouble, appealing to Sir Frederick, as many a one did, might be always sure of a ready hand and a tender heart.[25]

In this regard one notices from the Church Registers how assiduous he was in personally administering baptism, in an age when it would not have been thought wrong for such as himself to pass this duty to an assistant. More often than not one finds the father's occupation as 'labourer', and there are not a few sad entries, 'father unknown'.

Within the College itself, taking no part either in their school work or their training as choristers, Ouseley was necessarily a shade remote from the boys. But not so remote that he had no contact with them and no regard, or that they did not come to know him. He made himself personally responsible for their preparation for confirmation; and there is ample evidence of his trouble in correspondence with them afterwards.[26] And he was not above sharing high spirits with them. In his reminiscences already quoted, Mr H.C.Lahee tells how one day the boys divided into two lines on opposite sides of the hall while Sir Frederick and the Headmaster (Millard) had a leapfrog race over them. Perhaps in a way they took the place of a family. Reminiscences of his Old Boys implicitly reveal affection and admiration for him and his unaffected friendly attitude to them.

No doubt some things imperfectly understood by boys may in after years have become garbled and exaggerated through the prism of age together with a certain accretion of sentimentality. Thus more than 50 years on one Old Boy averred his belief that Sir Frederick and Queen Victoria 'had been children together & playmates & up to the time of his death had access to her at almost any time'.[27] Hence a similar element of colourful exaggeration may contribute to their accounts of his extemporisation. Certainly there is reliable authority for his skill in that direction, though apparently confined to a contrapuntal style. But a picture of him and S. S. Wesley actually playing 'against each other' in this manner is hard to credit, whilst to say that 'at double fugues Sir Frederick could beat' Wesley is meaningless.[28]

Some allowance, then, may be necessary when reading M.F.Alderson's memories in Chapter 9. One begs leaves to doubt, for instance, that during term time 'hardly a week passed without visits from eminent statesmen, poets, diplomats, high ecclesiastics', and may feel some reservation about 'the rich stream which flowed from his master-mind'. Nevertheless, when all allowances have been made, there is something impressive about Alderson's devotion to Ouseley's memory, many times expressed, as several of us can still recall.

Tribute to him was more generally displayed when, in 1887-8, a group of Old Boys collected subscriptions for the cost of stained glass in the windows of the north aisle of St Michael's Church. Beneath these a small brass plate reads:

As a mark of respect to the Founder, and in remembrance of their school-days, the three windows in this aisle were given by former pupils of the College, Christmas, 1888.

They were not actually inserted until about the end of January 1889.[29] This was only just in time, for his death occurred suddenly at Hereford on 6 April. His body was brought to St Michael's for burial on 11 April in the place traditionally allotted to the founder of a church, outside and beneath the east window. The College choir was joined by that of Hereford Cathedral and representatives of Worcester Cathedral choir.[30] No fewer than 21 Old Boys attended at very short notice. In due course the grave was covered by a recumbent cross designed by (Sir) Aston Webb, with an inscription describing him as

Vicar of this Parish: Founder of the Church and College of St Michael and All Angels.

It is obvious that obituary notices scarcely knew what to make of his twin foundations. One (unidentified) simply said his purpose was to give a free education to eight, and all but free education to a further eight, 'sons of necessitous gentlemen' with a preference for sons of clergy. *The Church Times* said 'he was appointed warden of St Michael's College, where he founded a musical library of some 2,000 volumes', and two other church papers, (*The Guardian* and *The Record*), as well as *The Times*, expressed themselves similarly. *The Daily News* spoke of 'the chapel' adjoining the College. *The Daily Telegraph* ignored the College, speaking of Ouseley as a clergyman who 'discharged the function of a country vicar' and as a composer and practical musician. *The Illustrated London News* and *The Morning Post* alike referred to him as '*Vicar* of St Michael's *College*' (present writer's italics), and *The Musical Standard* described the College as 'the classical, mathematical, and choristers' foundation school'. Only *The Musical Times* came near to getting it right.[31]

Ouseley's death created a sudden though not unpredictable crisis for the College. It spelt the cessation of his financial subvention without which it could not have paid its way; and it raised the problem of a salary for a successor Warden. In announcing the vacancy the Fellows stated that there would be no stipend. In these circumstances they turned to the only man qualified to help them on whose loyalty they could completely rely: John Hampton (1834-1921), who was elected Warden in May 1889.[31] In accordance with the Trust Deed he also became Vicar of the parish.

As we have seen, following his connection with St Paul's, Knightsbridge and St Barnabas', Pimlico, Hampton went to Lovehill House to help Fyffe with Ouseley's group of boys there, and then proceeded to St Michael's to become Choirmaster at a salary of £120. In 1859, when in his 26th year, he went up to Queens' College, Cambridge, of which he was a scholar. But he did not sever his link with St Michael's, remaining on its books and apparently returning there in university vacations. Nevertheless his Cambridge years might have meant a turning point, for he was clearly a man of ability and energy, capable of carving a successful independent career. In his last term at Queens' he was offered a post as music master at Uppingham, and he recounted how Ouseley visited Cambridge to plead with him to remain at St Michael's. He offered him the curacy in addition to his position as Choirmaster with a further £120 salary, saying that if circumstances should make it impossible to pay that extra amount he would leave 'a round sum' (£7,000) in his will.

So Hampton threw in his lot with St Michael's following his ordination in 1862. There is no doubt at all that Ouseley leaned on him heavily. Hardly had the College begun than unexpectedly high building costs compelled retrenchment, and until going up to Cambridge Hampton supplied the place of second master without payment. On his return he received no remuneration as curate for about 20 years. In 1869 he was dignified with the appointment of Sub-warden, but this carried no salary. When one considers the numerous changes of Headmaster (to say nothing of the assistants) and Sir Frederick's unsuitability for direct control and administration, a good deal must obviously have been owed to Hampton as a continuous anchorage and adjutant over some 30 years. It was not that he had no chance to move had he so wished. Minor canonries and precentorships at Manchester, Bristol, and Worcester Cathedrals might have been his, and there was some discussion of Westminster Abbey. But it was to St Michael's that he gave his loyalty.[33]

While there his musical skill found additional outlet in his foundation of the Tenbury Musical Society which he conducted. Of course College musicians played their part, but it catered for the local amateur, stiffened as to the orchestra by some visitors and professionals. Among the last, at an early stage of his career, there was sometimes the young Edward Elgar, who remembered that it was at Tenbury under Hampton that he first came to know Dvorák's *The Spectre's Bride.*[34] The record of works performed under Hampton in these rural surroundings shows some catholicity and enterprise.[35] Elgar's regard for Hampton is perpetuated in the dedication of the partsong *My love dwelt in a northern land*, a masterpiece of its genre. It must be deplored that recent printings of this work by Messrs Novello & Co. omit the dedication legend.

Ouseley's will was found to bequeath not £7,000 but £8,000 to Hampton, a well-earned legacy indeed, whose recipient immediately devoted £1,000 to the College. After other personal legacies, the residue of the Founder's estate, in accordance with his wishes, formed a second Trust for the College, though its early benefit was small, the assets tied up in land. Nevertheless, after the initial panic in which notice had been given to the lay clerks, and an uneasy Summer Term, Hampton managed to carry on with an alto, a tenor, and a bass lay clerk, a Headmaster who was a 'fair bass', and an assistant master who was a 'very good tenor'. Help was given by a public appeal for an Ouseley Memorial Fund which raised a useful if not spectacular sum in support of the College. Then in 1892 Miss Georgina Rushout died, bequeathing £18,000 net on trust for the Church and College. At this point Hampton felt justified in claiming the Warden's stipend which, he said, 'was not very gladly given'.

In that year he married and moved out of the College into the vicarage. Ouseley had contented himself with a set of personal rooms forming part of the College buildings. Hampton's move as Warden represented his one substantial departure from his predecessor's regime. He was explicitly briefed to 'carry on exactly as Sir Frederick himself did and wished', and this he faithfully did.

One does not doubt that the standards of church music were maintained; and in the central part of his term of office, 1896-1907, he was well supported by the young organist, E. C. Broadhurst, a pupil of Sinclair. Of these days we have the personal recollections of Heathcote Statham (see Chapter 9). But the prestige of Ouseley's personal rank was removed along with his repute among church musicians (especially clerics) and the influence of his Oxford position. It would seem that St Michael's gradually receded from consciousness, and it is significant that the two accounts of it in contemporary journals both concentrate on Ouseley's antiquarian collection.[36] It was J. S. Bumpus's *History of English Cathedral Music*, published in 1908 and dedicated to Hampton, which to some extent revived knowledge of it and on which public understanding of it rested for many a long year.

From about the mid-1890s an annual feature of Commemoration Day was an afternoon organ recital by G. G. Sinclair. This detail is worth record because in 1906 his programme on 4 October included an arrangement (presumably his own) of the Prelude to Elgar's *The Kingdom*, a work which only the day before, in Birmingham Town Hall, had received its first performance. The series of celebrations in that year, marking the jubilee of the College, showed that whether or not its public fame had declined, it continued to command the loyalty *con amore* of those connected with it, and Hampton could feel reward for his long service and devotion.[37] By then he was already 72 years old. Eight years later the problems of a world war were added to his own increasing age and declining health. He resigned in 1916 and died in December 1921. His grave in the churchyard of St Michael's is next to that of the Founder. The Church clock, which gives the time both to the College and to passers-by on the road outside, was installed in his memory.

As his successor the Fellows elected the Revd G.C.E.Ryley, B Mus, MA, who for a short time some years earlier had been an assistant master. As a graduate in music he completely fulfilled the *desideratum* of the Statutes; but after only a few days residence ill health supervened and he was compelled to resign. The only function he appears to have discharged was to appoint two Fellows, one of them appropriately enough his predecessor as Warden. An interregnum of some months ensued during which Canon E.C.Corfe, an Old Boy, stepped into the breach until in June 1917 the reins were assumed by the Revd E.H.Swann, and a new era began.

CHAPTER 5

THE CHOIR REPERTORY UNDER OUSELEY

by the Editor

By 1850 there was a considerable amount of published church music from Elizabethan days onwards available for choirs. To the basic repertory of Boyce's *Cathedral Music* supplemented by that of Samuel Arnold, the more enterprising could add that of Page's *Harmonia Sacra* (3 vols, 1800). More recently the useful series (42 numbers) of standard services and anthems initiated by Goss and Turle in 1843, the group of services edited by William Marshall in 1844, and the resources of Rimbault's *Cathedral Music* (1847) had become available. In W.H.Cope's *Anthems by Eminent Composers for the English Church* (1849-51) 33 other items were accessible. In addition there were the 18th-century substantial albums of works by Croft, Greene, Boyce, William Hayes, and Philip Hayes. To this extensive classical resource Ouseley himself had added by his *Collection of Cathedral Services by English Masters* (1853) comprising Child in A minor, Church in F, Creighton in B flat, John [but attributed to Richard] Farrant in D minor, Kelway in G minor, Kempton in B flat, Rogers in E minor and in F, and Tomkins in C.

On top of this considerable repository from the past there was available the recent work of men slightly senior to or contemporary with Ouseley himself, of whom the chief were Elvey, Hopkins, Goss, Walmisley, and S.S.Wesley. In another ten to fifteen years there was the next generation of Garrett, Stainer, Sullivan, and others to draw on.

Ouseley himself made certain direct contributions to the enlargement of these various groups, and in the first place by the injection of a large proportion of his own music, both services and anthems. From what we know of him, we must acquit him of anything vainglorious in this, assuming rather that he felt the round of daily worship could be enriched by a choice of anthem texts which not infrequently broke new ground. However, by no means all his prolific output came into general use outside St Michael's.

A further personal contribution, again with an eye to specific texts, was his anthology of new music in *A Collection of Anthems for Certain Seasons and Festivals* in two volumes, 1861 and 1866. This drew on his contemporaries and immediate seniors as well as the next generation. He was himself the most extensive of the 23 contributors, and it was here that the still current *From the rising of the sun* and *Is it nothing to you* first appeared. Two other items, *O that I knew* (Sterndale Bennett) and *I saw the Lord* (Stainer), have shown staying power; and two more, *Blow ye the trumpet* (Henry Leslie) and *God came from Teman* (Charles Steggall), had considerable, if now largely exhausted, popularity. But though well intentioned, there was an unhappy mediocrity about these albums, notwithstanding the names of Goss, Hopkins, Elvey, Barnby, and Sullivan. Several of the contributors were nonentities and some must have been included solely on grounds of personal friendship, E.J. Ottley, for instance, and C.F. Fox Chawner, who spent several terms as an adult commoner at St Michael's before ordination and his early death.[1] And yet, one must ask, what other contributors could Ouseley have sought in this undistinguished period? But he seems not to have been over exacting in his artistic criteria for the purpose. Discussing his project with J.B. Dykes (who also contributed) he wrote on 8 January 1858:

> I feel sure that any musician who sits down to write a service or an anthem with the old Church composers before him as his model, & with an enthusiastic feeling of singlehearted devotion, beginning his work with prayer to God, & determining to admit nothing into it unworthy of the Sanctuary - I feel sure that anyone so acting will be in a fair way of producing something *really good*.[2]

The most distinguished contemporary church composer was not, however, represented. S.S. Wesley was evidently not attracted by the company he would keep. On 3 February 1858 he wrote:

> I regret to have to submit to you that I feel opposed to taking any part in your projected work. I should be always inclined to keep myself separate from the

> persons who will, no doubt, act in this matter... I fear the publication will do some harm. Your specimens ought to be *great*...It vexes me to resist your bidding thus.[3]

The third way by which Ouseley contributed to an extension of the repertory was his edition of *The Sacred Compositions of Orlando Gibbons* (1873), which aimed to present the complete *oeuvre* for the first time.

On the question of how he drew on this mass of material for his purposes at St Michael's, a comprehensive analysis of all the music sung there is beyond the present scope.[4] The following discussion is based merely on a rapid scanning of the data. But to support it with some objectivity, in Appendix F below the list for the last complete week in October (a time free from any marked conditions of the Church's year) for his first year, 1857, is set out for comparison with those at ten-year intervals, 1867, 1877, and 1887, the last only six months before his death. Further, in Appendix G details are given of the full year's repertory in 1865 (by which time the College was well set on its way) and again 20 years later in 1885.

On the evidence of the service lists, Ouseley's view of the music of the historic period from Tallis to Attwood placed the centre of gravity in the 18th century, with an extension to the late 17th century to take in the sober figures of Rogers and Aldrich. This reflects the proportions of what was available. Yet his acceptance of those proportions must be adjudged a matter of choice. He neglected some things which would slightly have adjusted that emphasis. For example, it is particularly striking that, while using Tallis's Short Service freely, he should have ignored that of Byrd. Richard Farrant's well-known Service in G minor he passed by, and that by Purcell in B flat seems not to have appealed to him at all. Again, though he himself had published Tomkins's Service in C, he made no practical use of it, and he took no opportunity to avail himself of Gibbons's Second Service after editing it in 1873. In 1878 he set himself to revise and transcribe a group of 'Ancient Cathedral Services'.[5] This is an interesting set, all of pre-Civil War date, and includes three works by Morley, two by Byrd, and one each by Ward, Parsons, and Ramsey. But he appears to have regarded the task as purely antiquarian, not related to the practical requirements of the Church of England in the 19th century, and he made no use of any of them with his choir. Some are 'verse' services. Can it be that he regarded these an inappropriate liturgically?

One recognises of course that there was simply not enough interesting music to provide services for more than 500 occasions a year. Yet it is curious to find such an intensely musical mind as Ouseley's accepting so freely the work of (say) Gates, leaning so heavily on King and Rogers, accepting Bryan (whose Service in G is by no means flawless) and being so fond of Kempton's demure setting. Moreover, his own services largely stem from the 18th-century type. This, then, may be what he considered liturgically proper. The two early 19th-century masterpieces which had boldly broken away from it, Walmisley's setting in D minor and S.S.Wesley's in E, were slow to gain admission to his repertory, and were never so much used as Goss in E. When he began to use the work of Stainer, Garrett, and other young men, the emphasis on the (to us) uninspiring work of the Rogers, King, Gates, Kempton, and Kelway group was but little reduced to make way for them. And his neglect of Byrd's Short Service, to which no liturgical exception whatever can be taken, remains wholly inexplicable.

The foregoing remarks apply to services, but much the same is true of anthems. What he used by Gibbons was mostly available before his own edition of 1873, which so far as his own choir was concerned resulted chiefly in the addition of *O all true faithful hearts* presented with the substitute words 'O thou the central orb' supplied by H.R.Bramley, and *This is the record of John*. Furthermore, though there was some good material of pre-Civil War date (by Tomkins, for example) available in Cope's collection, Ouseley virtually ignored it.[6] This seems to be contradicted by Heathcote Statham who, as one who became a chorister ten years after

Ouseley's death, recalled that they sang a good deal of '16th-century' church music. In this respect the choice of music was not much changed under Hampton's wardenship, and one can only suppose that as Statham recollects not liking that kind of music when a boy it seemed to him larger in bulk than it really was.

Among anthems of his own day, Ouseley certainly did not neglect those of S.S.Wesley, though he clearly preferred the tamer setting of *The Wilderness* by Goss. It is a little curious perhaps that *Cast me not away*, which after all is in a more purely ecclesiastical style of counterpoint than Wesley's other anthems, was very little used. Some of his masterpieces were too elaborate to be within reach of the St Michael's choir, but independent sections of them were freely used. However, not even *Ascribe unto the Lord*, well within its capacity, was ever sung complete.

The work of the youngest composers of Ouseley's day, Barnby, Sullivan, and so on, came later to be almost universally condemned. Yet he welcomed it without reserve. From the picture we have come to make of him (whether right or wrong), it seems incredible that he of all people could accept anything like Sullivan's *Sing, O heavens*. Was it a feeling that, though outside his own creative reach, this was a style to be welcomed, or was it deliberate tolerance? Though we may deplore a very great deal of this, surely he was right to welcome new developments rather than to dwell in the past. Yet, as to the past, did he not tolerate much that was characterless, like the work of William Hayes?

Our standpoint, knowledge, resources, and hence our taste, are all different from his. *De gustibus non est disputandum.* If we ask how his lists compared with those of cathedral and similar choirs at that time, it is impossible to answer for want of adequate data. If one may hazard a guess it would be that his were similar in character and proportions, though perhaps more extensive in content. All in all, it does not appear that he exerted any distinctive influence on the style, or on the general character of the repertory, of music for the choral service.

CHAPTER 6

UNDER WARDEN SWANN, 1917-36

by the Editor

Ernest Henry Swann (1869-1948) went up to Corpus Christi College, Cambridge, as Exhibitioner and Organ Scholar from St John's School, Leatherhead, and then became an assistant master at Great Yarmouth Grammar School. While there he was ordained and in due course he moved to Ripon Cathedral as a minor canon. He eventually became Precentor and also had experience of parochial work, the Cathedral being Ripon's parish church.[1] By such various qualifications he was therefore well suited to be Warden of St Michael's. And if, unlike Hampton, he enjoyed no inheritance of direct association with Sir Frederick Ouseley, he had a compensating advantage in seeing the institution from outside.

For the time was now fully ripe for change. The original buildings were in urgent need of attention. Internal plastering, improved plumbing and hot water supply, installation of electricity from a small private generator, and provision of a sanatorium: such practical matters were now taken in hand one by one. Inheriting a school of only 23 boys,[2] Swann saw that it could no longer justify itself educationally unless it were enlarged by the admission of more non-singing, fee-paying boys. This, no less than self-evident teaching requirements, called for extended classroom accommodation beyond the old-fashioned single schoolroom of former years. The latter was now converted to recreational use, and before long housed a model railway. An unpretentious new building was erected with classrooms and changing facilities on the ground floor and some simple bedrooms for masters above. It was carefully placed to avoid spoiling a view of the main College buildings and Church.

To pay for these developments most of Ouseley's remaining family possessions were sold, thus converting one kind of trust property into another. Engravings, silver, glass, Persian furniture, and 'other art treasures' as well as some few selected volumes from the non-musical library (for example, certain of Gould's famous ornithological works)[3] were thus disposed of. Increased revenue from some years of prosperity after this expansion also contributed, and enabled a reserve fund to be established. Even so some things were left undone, notably provision of an assembly hall and practice rooms for instrumental music. These were discussed but ruled out for lack of funds. But it should be said that one improvement was later promoted by some commendable self-help. In 1933 the efforts of masters and boys in carrying out the excavation brought down the cost of constructing a swimming bath from some £400 to under £100.[4]

Swann was also behind a desirable constitutional change. Whereas hitherto not only executive affairs but all questions of finance and policy had rested solely and exclusively with the Warden (subject to Trust requirements), larger matters were now dealt with by a newly formed Governing Body under him as chairman. At the same time the appointment of Fellows (who elected a majority of members of the Governing Body) ceased to be the prerogative of the Warden alone. These provisions were made in revised Statutes of 1921 which also removed some obsolete original provisions. The three nominations to Fellowships which Swann had already made on his own responsibility suggest an intention to bring the College to wider notice: W.H.Frere, Percy Buck, and E.H.Fellowes, men of acknowledged standing, were drawn from outside the intimate circle of the Founder and the College. Fellowes was now elected a Governor under the new arrangements, and in 1921 (Sir) Sydney Nicholson became a Fellow-Governor, the pair of them representing important aspects of church music.

These significant changes must not be taken to indicate any intention to weaken Ouseley's purpose of daily choral services. Their effect was to strengthen the College for that purpose, with which the new Warden was in complete sympathy and which he loyally and fully pursued. Until nearly the end of his time as Warden, Swann was himself

Choirmaster. In accordance with changing taste the feebler works of Sullivan and other later Victorians gave place to more recent compositions by men such as Bairstow and Harwood. Some of the duller 18th-century works were abandoned while at the same time the current revival of Elizabethan and early Stuart church music made itself felt. It was at Commemoration in 1923 that the evening canticles of William Byrd's *Great Service* received what may well have been their first rendering since the 17th century.[5] For a great part of his regime Swann could rely, in addition to what help the Headmaster and his assistants might give in the choir, on a permanent core of lay clerks, and in 1930 Mr George Coles was appointed as a 'junior' lay clerk, thus beginning his long and important service as a bass lasting more than 50 years. However, need for economy in the early 1930s not only meant dispensing with some lay clerks but also a reduction in the number of boys in the choir to 12.

It was left to Swann to take two steps from which Ouseley had shrunk. During the interregnum after Hampton's departure Canon Corfe had introduced a choral celebration of Holy Communion on Sunday mornings. Not only was this made permanent, but in 1920 eucharistic vestments were adopted. Swann also introduced cassocks and surplices for the choir, in place of the academic pattern of surplice (open down the front, buttoned at the neck, and worn without cassock, as familiar to lay foundationers of Oxford Colleges). Besides the choral celebration he had Morning Prayer with a parish choir raised and trained by him. For how many years this continued, one cannot say.

Another initiative taken by Swann, and in quite a different sphere, may have seemed small at the time but will certainly prove to have the most enduring results. The Founder's extensive collection of music and books on music was without any adequate catalogue and needed attention. It had not been any concern of the first Honorary Librarian, Mr J. S. Sidebotham. His successor, Mr J. S. Bumpus (probably appointed on Sidebotham's death in 1901), certainly interested himself in it but in an unsystematic way. Already during Ouseley's life it had begun to overflow from his study into various parts of the College. The new Warden at once grasped the importance of attending to it, and to that end, Bumpus having died in 1916, he appointed the Revd Surtees Talbot, Minor Canon of York Minster, to be Honorary Librarian. But Mr Talbot died before he could accomplish anything. In these circumstances Swann sensibly turned to Mr Barclay Squire of the British Museum for suggestions. Meeting Dr E. H. Fellowes after they had both attended the funeral of Sir Hubert Parry in St Paul's Cathedral in 1918, Squire asked whether he would undertake the duty. After hesitation (for he was heavily committed to his work on *The English Madrigal School*) Fellowes agreed. In the course of visits of some fortnight's duration each and sometimes working as long as 14 hours a day, by Michaelmas 1923 he had accomplished an immense task singlehanded and in an unpaid capacity. The volumes were brought together (some few even from the kitchen and the corridor leading to the dormitory), repaired and bound as necessary, arranged in reasonable order on extra shelving in the library proper, and catalogued.[6] The manuscripts, at that time numbering 1386 and some of them containing large numbers of items, were catalogued in book form, the printed material (well over 2,500 volumes) on cards. Ouseley, it is true, had collected the material; but it was Fellowes who created a library from it, and it was Swann who realised the College's responsibility towards it. In 1934 the *Catalogue of Manuscripts in the Library of St Michael's College, Tenbury* was published in a limited edition of 200 copies by Editions de l'Oiseau-lyre of Paris through the generosity of Mrs Louise B. M. Dyer. It has never proved possible to publish a catalogue of the printed material.

In the later part of the first World War short-term appointments as deputy organist had been made. In 1919 Swann secured the services of Dr Ernest Bullock on his demoblilisation. But in less than a year he left for Exeter Cathedral as a step in a career leading to Westminster Abbey and eventually to the post of Director of the Royal College of Music. He was succeeded at St Michael's by Heathcote

Statham, a gifted Old Boy. He composed a simple operetta, *The New Master*, for performance by boys and staff which was published by Curwen. This was revived after the second World War, but probably by now, when pretty advanced fare is tackled in schools, it would seem too unsophisticated for further revival. Statham also followed with interest Fellowes's work on the Music Library, and as a result, by putting together some early text surviving at St Michael's with other to be found in the Fitzwilliam Museum, Cambridge, he made an interesting contribution to church music by editing *Fourteen Full Anthems* by John Blow (O.U.P., 1925).

In 1928 Swann, recently widowed, remarried. His second wife, Miss Helen Young, had been trained at the Royal College of Music and she placed her skill both as singer and pianist at the disposal of the College. She also helped her husband in organising a parish choir for the vacations. When in 1931 an enterprising organist, Mr Laurence Crossthwaite, was appointed she readily responded to his initiative in some interesting directions. From this date there are several instances of her playing a piano concerto (or a movement from one) in the church to his accompaniment on the organ. In 1932 she took the female name- part in a production of *Dido and Aeneas*. In those days when musical activity in preparatory schools was usually minimal, such an enterprise, however appropriate to St Michael's, was wholly exceptional. To have staged even Purcell's short work in the College's small dining hall, so ill-adapted to any such purpose, must have been a triumph of determination. In the same year, at Commemoration, Crossthwaite organised a performance of Constant Lambert's *The Rio Grande* in the College library. A two-piano version was used, either Mrs Swann or the Headmaster (Mr T. P. Marsden) taking the taxing solo part, the other an arrangement of the string and brass orchestral part, while the battery of miscellaneous percussion instruments was resourcefully tackled by a guest player, Mr Stephen Moore, and the chorus was, of course, the College choir. In 1934 came a still more ambitious undertaking, a production of *The Magic Flute*, for which the Tenbury Drill Hall was requisitioned. Mrs Swann had the part of Pamino, the chorus and all other characters being found from boys and masters. A slight simplification of the demanding aria for the Queen of the Night was made for the boy soloist, and an adaptation of the orchestral score was made for a small ensemble of strings and woodwind, conducted by Crossthwaite.

Scant information is available about the careers of boys who passed through St Michael's during this period. What there is may be gleaned from news of Old Boys printed in later issues of the *St Michael's College Magazine*. With its choir scholarships (even though these no longer afforded complete exemption from fees as in Ouseley's day) one may suppose that there were many boys of musical aptitude; yet none achieved prominent distinction as practising musicians. Nevertheless there was a future Warden (Kemp-Welch) and a future Organist (Menzies) of the College. There was also a future clergyman, N.E.Wallbank (1924-29),later Rector of St Bartholomew's, Smithfield, London, who by taking the degree of Doctor of Music would surely have delighted the Founder's heart. As it happens the best known names are those of Commander Kingsmill Bates (1927-31), who played a prominent part in sinking the German pocket battleship *Scharnhorst* in December 1943; Christopher Grier (1933-36), music critic of the (London) *Evening Standard*; Christopher Hassall (1921-25), poet, librettist, and man of letters; Martin Maddan (1928-34), Member of Parliament; and Hilary Watts (1925-29), racing motor cyclist. Except Maddan, all had been in the College choir. It was these days under Swann that were so sensitively evoked in retrospect by Hassall in his delightful 'Poem for Michaelmas Day. Variations on a theme of Thomas Hood for the Centenary of St Michael's College, Tenbury' (see p.viii).

The College was not entirely without its troubles. It was unusual in that two officers who would normally have carried independent authority, the Headmaster and the Organist, were subject to the Warden who, as stated, also took charge of the choir. Matters were not improved by the very small size of the institution in which functions were thus divided. So friction arose. How things would have transpired had Ernest Bullock stayed longer than a few months one cannot say. As it was, it turned out unfortunately that these awkward dispositions should have affected Heathcote Statham, who was by now a Cambridge Doctor of Music. Like the Headmaster, he found his position irksome, and both were asked to leave. Perhaps with a musician of his attainments this was implicit in the arrangements of the College. They were eventually modified some two years before Swann's retirement, when he exchanged the post of Choirmaster for that of Headmaster in succession to Mr Marsden, whereupon the Organist took over the choir and a post of 'Second Master' was created as second-in-command to the Warden-Headmaster. Then there was some vacillation about this. Only a few months before Swann's departure he gave up as Headmaster whereupon the Second Master (Mr E.F.Collander Brown, who must have been forbearing) was 'provisionally' appointed.

The other trouble was finance and recruitment. After the success of Swann's first 14 years or so the Governing Body minutes give signs of much anxiety on these grounds. Hence the reduction in the number of choirboys just mentioned and other economies. The years from 1930 were, of course, a time of national financial difficulty and no doubt this may have been the initial cause of insufficient recruitment. However that may be, it was the beginning of a persistent symptom.

Nevertheless Swann breathed new vitality into the College, and the formative character of his wardenship needs no emphasis. Viewed in general it was a period of steady progress and sensible direction enabling the establishment to keep quietly on its way. He retired in January 1936 to become Vicar of Bridstow, near Ross-on-Wye. Fittingly, he lies buried in the churchyard beside Ouseley and Hampton.[7]

CHAPTER 7

THROUGH WAR TO THE CENTENARY, 1936-56

by the Editor

As Swann's successor the Fellows elected the Revd C.H.S.Buckmaster, Chaplain of Denstone College. The new Warden's wish coincided with the tentative experiment at the end of his predecessor's time. He absorbed the work of a headmaster into his post of Warden and he assumed direct control of the school, living in the wing of the College which had been Ouseley's. This was obviously a sensible policy on both administrative and financial grounds, and it was consistently followed thereafter. On the other hand it does not seem to have occurred to those responsible (or, if it did, they considered it unimportant) that by this decision future fields of candidates to have charge of the school would be restricted to clergymen, since the Warden was required to be in Holy Orders.

It confirmed and strengthened a change which, by natural development, had long been taking place in the appearance which St Michael's presented to the outside world. Ouseley's starting point had been a country parish church whose incumbent was also Warden of an establishment - choirmaster, organist, lay clerks, and a school for choir boys - to maintain in it daily choral worship of an exemplary kind. No doubt Hampton understood it in that way. But such a notion was so obviously unusual for such a parish that bit by bit the College must necessarily have begun to seem the starting point. This can only have been intensified as the number of non-singing boys increased, the activities of the College became more lively, and the demands of education more pressing, while even the nominal adherence of a rural flock to its parish church declined. So the Church came to seem like a college chapel; and indeed accounts of matters connected with the choir and church music under Swann regularly appeared in the *St Michael's College Magazine* with the heading 'Chapel Notes'. While nothing was changed in essence - and certainly Swann did not neglect his duties as

Vicar - there was gradually a subtle adjustment in what it is fashionable to call an 'image'. And now, under the new arrangement, the term 'Warden' which had hitherto dignified the Vicar of the parish decidedly came to look like a fancy title for a preparatory school headmaster. Church musicians interested in the College and parents of the boys were hardly conscious that he was the Vicar. Incidentally the constitutional anomaly was created whereby the Headmaster, sitting with the title of Warden, was chairman of his own Governing Body.

Correspondingly there is a change in our present subject matter. Earlier chapters may justify themselves perhaps by constituting a footnote to the history of 19th-century English ecclesiology. But, by a gradual process, the story has become simply the domestic one of a small school (albeit of special character), its administration, activities, and personalities, appealing mainly to those closely associated with it in recent years.

Before war broke out Mr Buckmaster was responsible for several improvements to the College buildings and amenities.[1] Then in 1940 he felt a call to serve as a naval chaplain, at which point it was fortunate that Dr A.V.Billen was available to become Acting Warden. He was a man of formidable intellectual achievements. As a Scholar of University College, Oxford, he had taken first classes in mathematics in both Moderations and Finals and he was also Senior Mathematical Scholar of the University. Later he took the University of London degrees of BD and Ph D, making his special study the Latin texts of the Old Testament which eventually secured him the Oxford DD degree. While teaching at Leeds Grammar School he was ordained and went on to become Headmaster of Ellesmere College and then of Wellingborough School. Supported in domestic affairs by Mrs Billen, he vigorously tackled his job and its additional wartime problems. Paradoxically, in spite of those difficulties, the College seemed to flourish. A significant factor was its position in what was considered a safe area in the event of air raids (this was the only period when its location was anything but a disadvantage). Conditions involved fluctuations and occasional gaps in the staff. Here Billen, an experienced schoolmaster, was a host in himself, well able to tackle mathematics and Latin, and of course Divinity and English, as required. He energetically organized the boys in various forms of useful war-time activity such as wood cutting. A characteristic personal touch was his introduction of one or two small elements of dignity. He insisted on the wearing of gowns by the Fellows (as the Statutes laid down) and when Bishop Parsons attended the College for the first time as its Visitor he was ceremoniously received *ad portam* with a Latin speech.[2]

Shortly before Mr Buckmaster arrived, Mr Maxwell Menzies, an Old Boy of Swann's time, had been appointed choirmaster and organist. When he now left for war service the College was again unusually fortunate in having Sir Sydney Nicholson and Mr C.E.S.Littlejohn to supply his place. And surprisingly enough it was found possible, though with frequent changes, to maintain a sufficiency of men's voices in the choir.[3]

At the end of the war Billen handed the College over in good heart with a useful list of prospective entrants, retiring to three successive livings within reach of Oxford and serving a period as Speaker's Lecturer in Biblical Studies in the University.[4]

An interesting production of the war years, even though it had nothing to do with the College's work, drew the attention of a limited circle of connoisseurs to its existence. This was *The Tenbury Letters*, edited by E.H.Fellowes and Edward Pine and published in handsome format on mould-made paper in a limited edition of 300 copies by the Golden Cockerell Press in 1942. It was a selection from a collection of about 250 autograph letters, assembled by Miss Mary Jane Ouseley, the Founder's sister, from well-known and important figures - royalty, statesmen, writers, scientists, etc., including Napoleon, the elder and younger Pitt, Horace Walpole, Rousseau, Ampère, and Queen Charlotte (wife of George III). The work of transcribing the letters for publication and a good deal of the annotation was that of Mr Edward Pine who was for a short time a particularly valued member of the teaching staff. The entire collection was subsequently advantageously sold. [5]

Within a year of his return from war service Mr Buckmaster decided to rejoin the Navy. But this spell was not too short for him to appoint to the teaching staff an Old Boy who was to give nearly 40 years of service to the College: Mr A.B.Demaus, who in addition to his teaching duties sang alto in the choir, at various times took charge of the Scout Troop, edited the *Magazine*, and was Honorary Secretary of the St Michael's College Society, besides adding a picturesqueness of presence to the College throughout that time.

To succeed Buckmaster the Fellows appointed another Old Boy, the Revd Noel Kemp-Welch. After having been head chorister under Swann, Kemp-Welch went on from Aldenham School to King's College, Cambridge as a choral scholar. After ordination he served for a time as a chaplain of King's and then had parish experience as Vicar of Chaddleworth and Fawley, Berks. In addition to his marked musical talent, his training at St Michael's and Cambridge admirably suited him to maintain the tradition of priest-musician as Warden, and his beautiful rendering of the priest's part in the services was a feature of his regime. In the College which he took over there were two boys in the choir who later achieved musical distinction: Christopher Keyte and Christopher Robinson (both 1943-49), the former becoming a well-known bass singer, the latter organist in succession of Worcester Cathedral and St George's Chapel, Windsor Castle. They were followed by Jonathan Harvey (1949-52), now Professor of Music, University of Sussex, and an acclaimed composer. A non-chorister of later renown in another field was Colonel J.N.Blashford Snell (1947-49).

It was under Mr Kemp-Welch that the College's responsibility for the conservation of the Music Library was dealt with. This had long been stressed by Fellowes, who had interested the Pilgrim Trust in it. At first a fire-proof addition to the main College buildings and uniform with them was considered, but this was too expensive in spite of a very handsome grant from the Pilgrim Trust and a further generous donation from an American lady who had no connection with the College. The Warden then had the idea of a fire-proof chamber constructed within the recreation room (the old schoolroom). This was carried out by Messrs Chatwood in 1955 and a communicating door made through an interior wall of the library proper. To compensate for accommodation thus lost, a prefabricated recreation hall was constructed away from the main buildings. If by no means an architectural treasure, this was a good exchange affording more ample space. Some years later it was equipped as a useful theatre, largely by the amateur craftsman's skill of Mr Michael Oldroyd who taught mathematics and, as an ex-choral scholar of King's College, Cambridge, was a valued member of the choir. Meanwhile, looking ahead, Mr Kemp-Welch had been raising funds to mark the coming centenary of St Michael's by a thorough overhaul of the splendid 4-manual organ in the Church, and this too was accomplished in 1955.

An unusual musical event for which he and his wife were chiefly responsible was a series of performances of Britten's *Let's Make an Opera* in the summer of 1951. For this the big dormitory was temporarily converted into a theatre while the boys slept in tents. It was professionally produced by Anne Wood who (understudied by Miss Smallman, a member of staff) took the part of Miss Baggott. All other parts were supplied from within the College. Mrs Kemp-Welch, on this and other occasions ready to use her singing voice to the advantage of College activities, took the part of Rowan. Mr Menzies, who conducted, trained the boys, and they had the benefit of a visit from the composer at a preliminary stage. The accompaniment was in piano duet form in which the Warden bore an expert part.

For the centenary celebrations of September 1956 Mr Kemp-Welch, in collaboration with the Organist (Mr Kenneth Beard), planned the music for a series of five services beginning with the eve of Michaelmas and continuing through the following two days. Benjamin Britten specially composed his beautiful *Antiphon* (words by George Herbert) for the occasion and thus the music of the celebrations ranged in chronology from Byrd to Britten. It was also representative of many musicians who, as Wardens, Fellows, Organists, or Old Boys had contributed something to the music of the English church. Fittingly, it began with *Give us the wings of faith to rise* as an introit in Sir Ernest Bullock's setting and closed with a new Te Deum by Heathcote Statham. As Visitor of the College the Bishop of Hereford presided at the Sung Eucharist on Michaelmas Day when the preacher was the Dean of York (Eric Milner-White); at the concluding Evensong the next day he himself preached in his capacity as Diocesan, so emphasising that it was the centenary not only of St Michael's College but of St Michael's Church also.

The event was appreciatively noticed in such diverse secular journals as *The Manchester Guardian*, *The Scotsman*, and *The Times*, the last also publishing a general article on the College and its Founder (mis-called 'Gore-Ouseley') by its chief music critic. *The Manchester Guardian* was notable for the fulness of its information and grasp of the College's character. There may be food for thought in that, by contrast, *The Church Times* printed only a derisorily meagre few lines until, after a week or two, Dr Henry Coleman (formerly Organist of Peterborough Cathedral) wrote in vigorous protest at this treatment.

The centenary services were conducted by Warden Kemp-Welch, although he had in fact just begun his new work at St Peter's School, York. When they were over the College and parish settled down to await his successor, who took charge in January 1957.

CHAPTER 8

The Latest Years, 1957-85

by the Editor

Following the centenary a constitutional anomaly was eliminated. The Warden now ceased to be ex-officio chairman of the Governing Body, though of course he normally continued to take part in its deliberations. The first chairman was then Colonel W.R.Prescott of nearby Bockleton Court, an immensely respected figure of the County whose integrity and balanced judgment in times of perplexity were of the greatest value. In due time he was succeeded first by Dean Seiriol Evans and then by an Old Boy, Mr H.G.Pitt, Vice-Provost of Worcester College, Oxford.

Each of the three succeeding Warden-Headmasters covering the next 29 years imparted his personal style to the College, and each brought his individual ideas, initiative, and effort to the task before him. But there is an underlying unity to the years 1957-85 in the consistent nature of that task - to save the College by building around it a flourishing preparatory school (the only means by which it could survive) while at the same time preserving its fundamental purpose. We shall return to this basic problem. Meanwhile, at the end of Mr Kemp-Welch's time there were those who, not without influence, saw it more simply: that of building up a flourishing preparatory school while minimising the original purpose. That might or might not have succeeded. But was it the right solution? Be that as it may, this view did not prevail, and in the Revd D.W.A.Stride a Warden was found prepared to attempt the balancing act. He came from Dover College where he had been Chaplain and had acquired experience as a Housemaster which was valuable in his new post. Not himself a musician, he yet grasped the central place occupied at St Michael's by the choral services which he never ceased to maintain with dignity. Rightly perceiving that he could confidently rely on the Organist to maintain musical standards, he addressed his efforts primarily to the educational work of the school and was successful in arresting the decline in recruitment which had once more begun to show itself.

Mr Stride's successor was the Revd D.J.Paxman, who had been Chaplain of Solihull School. During his time, and with his approval, steps were taken to throw open future appointments as Warden-Headmaster to clergy and laity alike. To facilitate this the Bishop of Hereford understandingly collaborated to arrange, in the event of a lay Warden, for a joint appointment of a chaplain and assistant master in the College who should also be Priest-in-charge of the parish. This took effect when, out of a field of candidates both clerical and lay, Mr Andrew Walters was elected to succeed Mr Paxman. Having been joint Headmaster of Stubbington House School he brought for the first time to the post of Warden vital experience of work in a preparatory school. After leaving school (Ellesmere College) he had at first gone into business, but presently felt a vocation for teaching and so qualified at St Luke's College, Exeter. As College chaplain and Priest-in-charge of St Michael's Church the Revd G.A.H.Atkins was appointed, and he also undertook the teaching of Latin. Thus, in a roundabout way, though with a different division of labour, the dual control (as it used to be called) of pre-Buckmaster days was revived; but instead of a Warden-Vicar with a separate Headmaster there was now a Warden-Headmaster with a separate Priest-in-charge (like a vicar) who had jurisdiction over the parish church. Fortunately, good sense made the system work. Mr Walters's ordination after his appointment made no difference to this disposition of responsibility.

There is a tradition in the College that Ouseley designed the post of Organist as a kind of apprenticeship under the Warden. But now that the Warden was no longer expected to be a musician, far greater responsibility devolved on the Organist. At the time the work of Choirmaster was joined to his duties, Mr Crossthwaite was well qualified for it. As the list in Appendix J below shows, since that time all the Organists have been university-trained, nearly always through the 'Oxbridge' organ scholar system. All of them, though appointed at a young age and in some instances without previous experience of the kind, have shown high standards and responsibility. But there was one conspicuous lack in the attractiveness of the post. Having no assistant, the Organist was unable to get away during term time to be in touch with other professional music making, to give an occasional recital, or to attend a conference. This isolated him, cut off from stimulating or challenging contacts. At a rather late stage something was done to mitigate this by the appointment of a series of young men who, between finishing at school and taking up an 'Oxbridge' organ scholarship, could benefit by a useful apprenticeship under Mr Judd. Thus, for some months of the years at least, he thereby had some assistance; and they proved stimulating youthful members of the community.

In 1957 Miss Kathleen ('Katie') Ashley, who for some 35 years had been responsible for teaching French, retired from the College. I have not traced any record of the precise year when she began, but the Governing Body minutes of May 1924 note the increase of her salary [*sic*] from £80 to £90 a year (plus, of course, board and lodging). Not only had her long service rendered her a College character: she had earned the deep esteem of generation after generation of boys and gave stability in time of change. Outside the classroom she was a vigorous Cub leader and for very many years she was Secretary of the St Michael's College Society. In the following academic year Mr John Gray joined the staff, though not in direct replacement of her. For over a quarter of a century, by his versatile ability, especially in art and crafts and as a Pioneer leader, he too contributed a great deal to the College.

The problem of staffing was no light burden to the Wardens. In times past there were always young men to be found who, for board and lodging and a few pounds a week would spend two or three years in 'prep' schoolmastering without thought of making it a career. With increasing professionalism those days were over; and St Michael's could in no way match the Burnham Scale of salaries. Moreover, there was the question of men's voices in the choir. The neighbourhood offered little or no additional employment to attract lay clerks of the standard of cultivated musicianship now required. In post-war years only for a brief period (1954-59) were there as many as two besides Mr Coles: Mr Alan Thorpe (bass) and Mr Vincent Petley (tenor). Both were local residents who sang more for the satisfaction of it than as a means of remuneration. Mr Thorpe left for Southwell Cathedral in 1959, but Mr Petley continued almost until his death in 1981. Other singers had to be supplied within a tiny teaching staff which must also provide for supervisory duties while the choir was at work. On losing a tenor singer who taught French and coached cricket (say), a Warden might be faced with one who could teach not French but mathematics and was no good at cricket. Or he might find an excellent French master whose voice and musical skill was unacceptable to the Organist. Not only did this impose restraints on the recruitment of the ideal teacher or the ideal singer and involved some thin patches, but it called for continuous resource and elasticity in the planning of duties. As to teachers' salaries, Mr Paxman managed, by progressive steps, to bring them more nearly into line with the Burnham Scale, but the College was never able completely to match it.

No one without knowledge of this would have guessed it from the record of College life and activity as reported year after year in the *St Michael's College Magazine*. While some appointments were less successful than others and some were shortlived, a sufficient number of teachers (both men and women) devoted themselves whole-heartedly to it. Plays, Scouts (and, later, Pioneers), camping, team games, expeditions, and hobbies of various kinds all disclose a school which, though small, was pulsing with life. And in the field of scholarships and exhibitions it had no reason to hang its head. Selecting arbitrarily the last 15 years of its existence, boys and girls from the College obtained 14 academic awards, 7 art awards, and 35 music awards.

But underlying everything there was insecurity. Under the circumstances something even more was necessary to save the College than to run an active, happy, and educationally useful school. The first deficiency was the inadequate endowment of the primary church music side of its work, and next was lack of capital to promote improved facilities.

This needed more than an aggregation of gifts, however generous, from the College's own circle. Accordingly in 1960, with an eye to the resources of industry and the larger charitable trusts, an Appeal was placed in the hands of a professional fund-raising firm of good repute which was confident of satisfactory results. Mr Meredith Davies, a Fellow, enlisted the interest of Lord Harewood to be Patron. Benjamin Britten once more helped the College by becoming a Sponsor, and the Warden secured John Betjeman as another. But a rude shock ensued. St Michael's aroused warm loyalty in some of its Old Boys, and it made its sentimental appeal to *afficionados* of English church music; but in industry and the big fund-disposing charities it aroused nothing at all, despite the distinguished patronage and sponsorship. The professional fund-raising failed completely. The cause of church music did not achieve ready response in connection with an institution which lacked support in the form of the civic pride of a surrounding city or the appeal of some magnificent historic building. Refusing to be daunted, the College persisted in the Appeal itself, and with the aid of a network of Old Boys and parents, much individual generosity, and helpful contacts through certain Fellows, a total sum of about £30,000 plus nearly £7,000 for building extensions was raised by 1965.

The benefit of this did not make itself felt until after Mr Stride had left. Though £60,000 had been hoped for, it was nevertheless a sizeable sum in terms of those days, although unhappily soon rendered less significant by rapidly rising inflation. But it helped. And with the addition of a bequest (about £8,000) from Canon M.F.Alderson who died in 1961, another classroom block was built, much more in accordance with contemporary educational ideas, while the former 'new' building was equipped with facilities for science teaching and improved in other ways. Fittingly, the extra building was called after Canon Alderson, and it was formally opened by Mrs E.H.Swann in 1966, whereupon the classroom block erected in her husband's time was renamed the Swann Building.

Mr Paxman in turn rightly urged the need to add a Music School to the buildings. St Michael's stood for music, yet had woefully inadequate facilities with which to hold its own now that preparatory schools generally, unlike former days, were making a feature of it. So more fund-raising was undertaken and an excellent addition to the premises, comprising a concert hall, teaching rooms, practice rooms, and an instrument store, was made in 1971, officially opened by Lord Redcliffe-Maud.

One further development took place during his regime. Hitherto boys only had been admitted. One or two parents, however, rather than have son and daughter at separate schools, enquired about the possible admission of girls. This seemed a legitimate need which, if met, might increase recruitment. Suitable domestic adaptations were made and the school became a mixed one, though girls were always in a minority.

The valuable results of all these efforts were not enough in themselves to save the College. There was yet another deficiency: ends still could not be met without increased recruitment of full fee-paying pupils. And whatever teachers thought about it, the so-called 'Houghton' salary award of the early 1970's imposed a heavy strain on St Michael's in the effort to keep up with it, though not completely to match it. So in spite of everything he and his predecessors had done, finance and consequently recruitment at the end of Mr Paxman's time were an anxiety. It was for this reason, as already explained, that his successor was chosen from the widest field of choice of both clergymen and laymen. In taking up the post Mr Walters knew what a decisive challenge he faced and accepted it with zest. There was a general feeling that the ensuing five years or so would be crucial and that while he was exerting his best efforts finance must be made available to support the deficit meanwhile.

Among those without intimate knowledge there were some who from time to time expressed surprise that so valuable an asset as the Music Library was not sold for the benefit of the College. The fact was - and the trustees were warned of this by the opinion of learned Counsel whom they consulted on the point - that very considerable restraint was imposed on the Trust in this regard by Sir Frederick Ouseley's will. They were therefore never called upon to consider the agonizing question of what their attitude to the whole of the Music Library would otherwise have been. However, it appeared that the 'Toulouse-Philidor' Collection (see Chapter 10) which formed a part of it as acquired by Ouseley was free from that restraint. Moreover a small though valuable element which was required to render it complete had been purchased by the College after his death from its disposable balance. Bearing these matters in mind in relation to current needs, and considering also that this part of the Music Library could be detached from the whole without detriment to the integrity of what remained (with which it had no link of subject matter or provenance), it was decided to sell it along with items from the non-musical Library in order to help save the College. Without the investment income arising from the capital sum thus obtained the College could not have sustained the few succeeding years of endeavour to attract the *sine qua non* of more full fee-paying pupils.

At the same time the Governing Body, by now largely refreshed with minds free from recollection of the Appeal of the 1960s, decided on a further public Appeal. This time, though professional advice was obtained about the manner in which it should be conducted, it was administered by a committee in which Old Boys together with parents of past and present boys played an active part. Sir Adrian Boult consented to be President and a member of staff, Mr Peter Scott, heroically undertook to be Honorary Secretary.

Friends and admirers of the College again responded generously (some of them having already subscribed some 15 years earlier), but industry and the greater trusts proved almost impervious.

A more modest enterprise was the formation in 1979 of a small body of 'Friends of St Michael's College' whose funds made possible the purchase of some very useful pieces of equipment for the school.

While all this was going on the Warden, whose buoyant hope was not just to build up numbers enough to make ends meet but to enlarge the College, set about his task of recruitment by making it better known. He seized every chance of forging links with the town of Tenbury, and opportunities were extended for boys and girls to use College facilities for art and music on Saturday mornings, by which it was hoped to spread knowledge and dispel mysteries about St Michael's. It played host to all manner of bodies, from organists' associations to Daimler and Jaguar promotional dinners. Every deanery in the dioceses of Hereford and Worcester received an individual invitation to visit the College. The Warden sought every opportunity and neglected none to speak about the College to societies and groups of all kinds. With his encouragement Mr Judd accepted outside engagements for the choir, and Mr Judd also made two successful gramophone records of the choir (one of them made possible by sponsorship secured by a parent) which were widely praised. Mr Roy Massey, a Fellow, was good enough to associate the College with events in the Hereford 'Three Choirs' Festivals of 1979 and 1982. The most imaginative effort was an exceedingly attractive stand mounted during 'Expo 84' in the Birmingham International Exhibition Centre. Some loyal parents backed the Warden up in keeping this continuously manned. Visitors showed what seemed to be great interest and were invited to give their names and addresses, so that subsequently each received a personal invitation to visit the College. The response was chilling.

It had long been realised that publicity for the College must stress that, quite apart from the choir, it provided a sound and successful preparatory school education for boys (and girls) who were not in the choir. Every effort had been made to do this ever since the Centenary, and Mr Walters pressed ahead in the same way. But it may not unfairly be observed that where St Michael's was concerned some implacable obstacles had to be faced.

When appeals were made specifically for its endowment they must needs stress music and the choral services, reinforcing those aspects in the public mind, associated as they were with the musical prestige of people like Britten and Boult. There is also the unquestionable fact that the normal activities of one preparatory school among many, however admirable, are not news. When St Michael's came into the public eye it was usually on some musical account - a broadcast Evensong or a gramophone record. And if the question was posed, 'Why should St Michael's claim to be supported rather than any other preparatory school?' the answer could not do other than to refer to the choir and the daily choral services. The notion that it was chiefly a school for musical boys had got itself deeply lodged into such limited public consciousness of it as there was. It was not unknown for an Old Boy, who should surely have known better, to say that as his son was not musical he would not be sending him to St Michael's. Some notions have a vitality independent of the facts; and everyone knows how the public will persist in many an image even when brought face to face with its inaccuracy. So it was an uphill struggle. And in spite of the establishment of a pre-preparatory department which it was hoped might feed the upper school, recruitment, far from improving, showed signs of decline.

The time came when, looking not very far ahead, it was evident that a point would be reached at which the College would have a deficit which it could not discharge. The only resource for meeting the year-by-year deficits which were being incurred was the reserve fund dating from the 1920s, and this was now nearing exhaustion. The College's permanent assets, whether investments or property, being held on a charitable trust, could not be used for such a purpose. A particularly awkward difficulty was that however much it might want to signal distress to its friends it could not do so for fear of jeopardising the recruiting effort and making prospective parents, as well as current ones, feel doubtful.

At this point a possible solution presented itself which seemed to have much to commend it. A proposal was received that the College should move and become a junior choir house to an established independent school. After prolonged and hopeful negotiations it became apparent at the last that an important legal point would preclude the Charity Commission from giving the required consent, and the idea had to be abandoned. Thus a year went by during which, by the desire of the other party (beside obvious other objections), nothing could be said, and matters were now very serious indeed. That was in the summer of 1983 when there was just enough reserve to meet one more year's deficit, after which it would be unsecured.

Maybe it would have been well to have brought the College to a close in the summer of 1984. But the Warden refused to give up hope; and however bleak the outlook, those concerned felt that they could not but make possible one more year's effort. If only five pupils paying full fees could be recruited! Surely there was a duty not to give in just yet! But to make possible that further year's effort some exceedingly painful economies had to be inflicted.

After two more terms it was clear that closure was inevitable, whereupon the chief consideration became the dignity by which it was to be carried out. There had been two instances locally of schools which had closed without any notice at all, and this the Governing Body was determined to avoid. First the staff was told, having already been confidentially given some indication of how matters stood; then a term's notice was given to the pupils' parents. All possible assistance was given in finding places at other schools, and nearly every boy holding a choral scholarship was able to obtain a similar or better one elsewhere. On Sunday, 14 July 1985 a closing Thanksgiving

Service was held with a crowded congregation in St Michael's Church, the Warden being celebrant, the Bishop of Hereford the preacher, and the choir augmented by many ex-choristers. The message from the Archbishop of Canterbury printed on p.115 was read from the pulpit; and when, on returning to the cloisters at the conclusion, the head chorister recited the customary prayer, 'Pardon, O Lord, all that Thou hast seen amiss in this our service, and give us grace to worship Thee more worthily', the work but not the influence of St Michael's College, Tenbury came to its end.

O † O † O † O

POSTSCRIPT TO CHAPTER 8. After much careful consideration the Trusts for St Michael's College were eventually united in a Scheme made by the Charity Commission for England and Wales and entitled 'The Ouseley Trust', the income from which is to be applied 'for the purposes of promoting and maintaining to a high standard the choral services of the Church of England (whether simple or elaborate) ... including (but without prejudice to the generality of the foregoing) promoting the religious, musical, and secular education of pupils attending any school in which instruction in the doctrines of the Church of England is given and performance of the choral liturgy of the Church of England is observed'.

CHAPTER 9
REMINISCENCES

(a) by M. F. Alderson

(Montague Frederick Alderson was a boy at St Michael's College 1878-83. His father was a Canon of Peterborough Cathedral and Chaplain to the Queen; his paternal aunt was Marchioness of Salisbury, wife of the Prime Minister. He himself was Rector successively of Lutterworth, Leics., and Bemerton, Wilts, and latterly Canon (non-residentiary) of Salisbury Cathedral. A natural musician, he held the Oxford B Mus degree. He became a Fellow of the College in 1922 and died in 1962.)

I remember arriving, after a long and exhausting journey from London with my parents, on the afternoon of my first Michaelmas celebration, and being pitchforked, without rehearsal or other initiation, into my place in the choir. We wore no cassocks in those days, but long, full-gathered surplices of a coarse linen material and opened down the front, such as members of Christ Church, Oxford (which was Ouseley's college) are still accustomed to wear on Sundays. I could not have been of much use on that occasion, but I remember with awe and wonder the white-robed singers around me and the stringed orchestra in front of our stalls, and above all 'the Bart.', resplendent in his Doctor of Music robes, sitting in his stall and singing alto just behind me. He usually wore at service his MA hood and only his musical robes on special occasions. He kept these always carefully rolled up with his priest's stole of black fabric and placed them in a narrow ledge beside his writing table in his private library and study in his Warden's lodgings.

After service we adjourned to the College hall, and I took tea with my future companions, whose acquaintance I now made for the first time. I slept through that night in a cubicle of the large school dormitory feeling very unhappy and lonely. This soon passed, and I think those five years proved to be the happiest of my life. All the boys were friendly, and continued so long after, even when other schools and interests claimed us.

Here let me say at once that Ouseley's chief aim and object in life was to make the worship of the collegiate church [see p. 34 - Editor] of his own foundation the focal point around which all other interests revolved. He made us, little boys as we were, to feel that we must put our whole being into this discharge of this Duty to God, and he inspired us with the beauty of this offering which we were called upon to make. Of course the music - the best of its kind at that time - made us love the august Prayer Book services which must have been highly incomprehensible to our youthful minds. How well I remember once protesting on the paucity of the general congregation (often consisting of two or three elderly people), to be sharply rebuked for my lack of understanding that we sang to the honour and praise of God and in the invisible presence of His Holy Angels. That privilege on our part could not be too highly prized, and I cannot call to remembrance on any occasion any need on the part of authority to rebuke a chorister for inattention or disorderly conduct.

And so we carried on during term time. The terms were unusual even for those days. Ouseley, true to the scheme laid down in the Book of Common Prayer, desired that the Holy Days as well as the Great Festivals should not be prætermitted by the choir. Accordingly we had only two annual terms, with a holiday break after Christmas and in the height of the summer. Many parents used to protest, as in the case of large families brothers and sisters rarely saw each other from one year's end to another. But Ouseley was adamant. God's service precedes all domestic and family claims and ties; and so great was our parents' love of the College that they were ready to make the sacrifice. In my case, as in that of others, the difficulty was overcome by long visits of one's brothers and sisters (often accompanied by their nurses) to Tenbury, lodging in the farmhouses and cottages of the neighbourhood. This greatly mitigated what might otherwise have been regarded as unnatural hardship.

Moreover, the whole neighbourhood was friendly, hospitable, and interested in us, and I am sure we must have been at times a sore trial to them. Bird's nesting, trampling over hay grass, breaking down hedges, and the temptation which surrounding orchards at harvest time could be to a little boy who was not well fed and was often hungry, proved irresistible. But, as the kindly Herefordshire folk used to say, they got in return for their losses beautiful singing of little angels of which they were truly proud. There were occasions when tolerance was definitely abused and authority had to intervene and dire punishment descended. But, as far as I recollect, these were very rare and I am sure we deserved most richly the corporal punishment unhesitatingly meted out to us.

Although Tenbury was situated in such a remote part of the country it must not be assumed that life there was lacking in interest or novelty. During term time hardly a week passed without visits from eminent statesmen, poets, diplomats, high ecclesiastics and, above all, of musicians. Ouseley was a man of many parts, and he had from early life been brought into close contact with all and sundry. He had played duets with Queen Victoria and Mendelssohn [see p. 10 - Ed.]; his connection with Oxford had forged many intimate links between him and the leading figures of the ancient seats of learning.

The musical professors of other universities were numbered among his intimate friends: Sterndale Bennett of Cambridge, Sir Robert Stewart of Dublin, Sir Herbert Oakeley of Edinburgh. The last-named was the author of the memoir of Ouseley contributed to *Grove's Dictionary of Music and Musicians.* Sir George Grove himself was a visitor to Tenbury, and he set a high value on Ouseley as a writer on technical matters in his dictionary.

Great preachers of his time, notably Bishop Samuel Wilberforce, Dr Liddon, Dean Kitchin, Canons Knox Little and Scott Holland were invited to come and address us at the Michaelmas Commemoration; musicians, even some of European fame, such as Jenny Lind and her husband Otto Goldschmidt (founder of the Bach Choir), Charles Gounod, Sir Joseph Barnby, Henry Leslie could be seen walking about with him in our Herefordshire lanes and fields; and of all men he truly practised the apostolic injunction in being 'given to hospitality'. St Michael's was then the veritable Mecca for all who wished to avail themselves of the charming society of an ideal host or to study at first hand the best types of Anglican Church devotion.

Yet it was all so natural, with an entire absence of pose or effort. Everything seemed to grow like the plants of a well-ordered garden in their native soil; and if, in the rendering of the choir music a professional polish of more recent age was absent, the unique opportunity of studying things under the hand of a genius and enthusiast was our privilege and joy. Nowhere else had boys such advantages as were ours. On looking back, I for one deeply regret how, miserably unworthy, I must have disappointed him in failing to appreciate adequately the rich stream which flowed from his master-mind or from his magical fingers. (By-the-bye, I learnt later that he was double-jointed in hands and feet, which may have largely accounted for this.) No one of my knowledge ever since was able to throw himself so completely into the youthful mind or to put his rich store of experience so attractively at the disposal of all companies. Those large, penetrating eyes of his seemed to read you through and through; the simple dignity of his conversation, while it entirely put you at your ease, never permitted you to take liberties or to dare familiarities. You were ever conscious of the widest gulf between your understanding and his. Yet, with all his extraordinary talents (both mental and physical), he was, like Moses, 'the meekest of men'; and that seemed to attract him unfailingly to the youthful heart.

Then to turn to reminiscences of a lighter, perhaps a frivolous, vein, Sir Frederick had wonderful power of sleight of hand, performing marvellous card tricks to the delight of young parties. Indeed it was jokingly said that if he had not been what he was he might have made his fortune in such ways. Sound was woven into his very being; he always sang the scale as he rushed up and down the stairs. And what a range his voice had! He loved to show us how he could sing three entire octaves easily. He had a very impatient temper. On one occasion, whilst playing croquet on the lawn in front of the College, he threw his mallet over the trees and had to send Hill, the butler, to fetch it back. Or, again, in the vestry he tore his square cap to fragments - the outward sign of his horror and indignation at some boy being a few seconds late for chapel. On one occasion, when the pitch dropped slightly in the Litany, he (already intoning on A) rose a minor third, much to the consternation of the tenors and basses, to show his disapproval of the action of the choir. Nevertheless, in spite of all these indiscretions and sudden outbursts we loved him all the more.

I must refer to his dealing with older people as I saw it. Whenever he paid visits to friends, staying in their houses or even when dining out, he was invariably the centre of attraction, as a wide audience listened to his stories and delighted in his reminiscences on all topics; and if there was a piano in the room (and most hostesses took care to see that there was one at hand) he would start up from his seat and take his place at the keys and illustrate his words with his delightful playing. On these occasions the whole household staff would eagerly listen outside. He was so good-natured that he did not resent this. An appreciative audience of young and old made him the more ready to spend himself to the uttermost in giving them pleasure; but on looking back I think it must have prematurely worn his vitality out and hastened his end. He was only 64 years of age when he died.

When my voice broke and I passed on to Winchester he still continued his interest in my career. Nor was my case different from many another. He loved to keep in touch with his old boys, to write to them and to receive answers from them. One of the last of these which I received makes mention of the disease which subsequently killed him. 'I am suffering, so the doctor tells me, from a tired heart', he wrote. 'I hope it is not a bad heart'. When another signed himself as 'his former pupil' he replied with a tinge of sadness that he hoped it did not mean a permanent separation from his old master.

Nothing gave him greater pleasure than to welcome old boys for a visit to the old college; and as an ideal host he made one feel that he gladly and unstintingly placed himself at the disposal of such. He had the power as well as the ability to know what conversation would best interest, without giving the impression of talking down to another's level. How pleasantly as well as profitably did the days pass! Visits to the organ either at school or the cathedral; the perusal of his unique collection of autographs and scrapbooks; sometime exhibitions with comments on his library treasures; short walks; and then, in the evenings after supper (as in my case) pianoforte duets, in which he always took the treble part; and, best of all, his playing and singing one of his own oratorios or musical compositions interspersed with comments and explanations. I am sorry to say I never was able to attend one of his Oxford professorial lectures, although he told me that having held the post so long and being by statute required to give two every year he was hard put to it to find any fresh material for them. I believe the last of the series was on 'Spanish Music'. However, I never omitted to call upon him whenever he came up to Oxford. Here again he always seemed to be the centre of interest in any gathering and to be surrounded by a whole host of friends. Truly a sociable man in every sense of the word!

Lastly, how vividly I remember the shock on learning of his sudden death at Hereford. The light of one's young life seemed to have gone out. The potent influence of a spiritual and loving father had been withdrawn, and a personal bereavement had been sustained. It took some time to recover, and even at this lapse of time the impression remains.

Reprinted by permission from *The History of St Michael's College, Tenbury*, edited by M.F.Alderson and H.C.Colles (London, SPCK, 1943), pp.34-39, with the omission of purely introductory remarks. Note however that if Wilberforce and Liddon preached at St Michael's during these years it must have been on some occasion other than Commemoration.

(b) by Heathcote Statham

(Statham was a boy at St Michael's College 1899-1904. His father, H. Heathcote Statham, an architect, wrote an interesting book The Organ and its Position in Musical Art *(1909). For further biographical details see Appendix J.)*

I went to Tenbury in September, 1899, ten years after Ouseley's death. The Warden and Choirmaster was the Reverend John Hampton, who had been at the College since its foundation. A good deal has been written about Ouseley, but not enough, perhaps, about 'Hampy', as he was affectionately known to the boys. It is never easy, when a great figure goes, for his successor to fill his place. I do not think John Hampton made many changes from the Ouseley regime. He was an idealist, and I think his main concern was to see that the singing of the services was kept up to a high standard. In appearance he was the perfect figure of what a Warden of such a College should be; with a neat white beard, white tie, cutaway morning coat, and a hat that was a cross between a bowler and a top-hat. For some reason (probably the draught) he generally wore his hat at choir practice; and I have a clear picture of him (in my mind) seated, hatted, at the piano in the hall, surrounded by singing boys holding their folio copies of *Boyce*. He had an endearing way of going about his business at a quick trot, much in the way that Sir Henry Wood used to trot on to the platform at Queen's Hall. I think with both of them it was a sign of enthusiasm; of a desire to get on with the job. Certainly we boys loved and respected 'Hampy' and the College owes him a debt for keeping Ouseley's ideals alive at a difficult time.

The Organist when I was a boy was E.C.Broadhurst - now, happily and rightly, a Fellow of the College. He was a fine player, though we hardly ever heard him play a solo. We heard the beginning of his voluntaries, but by the time we reached the cloister we were out of range. I suppose that what we did *not* hear he played to an empty church. To play on he had a splendid four-manual Willis, blown by hand. For the services two gardeners worked the bellows, but I believe that on special occasions, such as a Sinclair recital, four people were needed to keep the wind supply going.

E.C.B. gave us our piano lessons. By an excellent rule every boy [in the choir - Editor] had to learn the piano, and had to practise for half an hour a day. The difficulty of fitting in the practice for sixteen boys was overcome by having half a dozen pianos down the middle of the big dormitory, so that half a dozen boys could play at the same time. Some of these pianos were old-fashioned square ones. The noise was shattering. E.C.B. would occasionally swim into this maelstrom of cacophony, having probably heard from downstairs that Jones minor was *not* playing his Bertini study in quite the orthodox manner. E.C.B. started me on the organ; and I remember gratefully that he did not sniff at my puerile efforts at composition, as he might well have done.

The main business of our life at College was, I suppose, to be choirboys and to sing the daily services. And sing them we did. Not a verse of the Psalms, not a suffrage of the Litany, not a prayer was omitted in those days. We sang, of course, to a completely empty Chapel; but that was, and still is, the charm of St Michael's - this singing of the daily offices in an empty church in the very depths of the country. I suppose there is nothing else quite like it in the world.

In addition to the boys, the choir in those days was made up of the Warden (tenor), two or three masters, and four lay clerks. The lay clerks were good. Barry Maund, the bass, was in his prime. He had one of those grand rumbling voices that reverberated comfortably on a low C. Perry Cox, the tenor, had one of the most beautiful voices that I have ever heard in a church choir. He was a wit, too, and a most faithful servant of the College. There were two altos, both good - Messrs Lowe and Williams.

What did we sing? A good deal of sixteenth-century church music; and very dull I found it. We sang it from our single part books, and we sang it in strict time, and in the right key. Tallis in the Dorian really *was* in the Dorian, and not a minor third higher. [By 'strict time' and 'the right key' the author is speaking of performance without the flexibility of accent and transposed notation which have since become generally accepted. - Editor.] Naturally we sang many of Ouseley's compositions, and some of these I found very dull too. I believe Ouseley too often suppressed his natural gift of melody from a misguided sense of duty: the duty of writing strict church music. But there were things that I enjoyed: *It came even to pass* was a superb noise; *And there was a pure river of water of life* I always thought very fine, and I believe that if I heard it again I should probably think so still. And there was his beautiful anthem *Jerusalem on high* from the oratorio *Hagar*, that is still sung at Michaelmas.

My musical taste, I am afraid, was deplorable. My favourite anthem (I really blush to write this in a journal connected with the RSCM) was Dykes's *These are they that came out of great tribulation*. Perhaps it was the enchantment of hearing Perry Cox sing 'Neither shall the sun light on them nor any heat'. Anyhow, it was my favourite! And my favourite setting? - Smart in B flat. Yes, I know, deplorable! But what boys like is rhythm, colour, excitement, and plenty of organ; and this old Smart gave them.

The great day of the year was, of course, Michaelmas. For one thing it was a day of feasting, when the boys could and did eat as much ham, pork, jellies, trifles, and so on, as they could manage. But it was the services that made the day. The choir was enlarged by many singers who were friends of the College, and in addition there was a quartet of string players from Birmingham. Always we would sing some big anthem or setting by Ouseley, and as every player and singer was a good musician we did it well. No-one (not even the boys who had never known him) could fail to be moved as they performed one of 'the Bart's' anthems in the Chapel that he had founded and loved. It was a Festival indeed, with the boys well breakfasted and well brushed, wearing those billowing surplices which voluminously cover the person and which look so romantic in Victorian pictures of choirboys, particularly if, in addition, a tactful beam of sunlight falls on boyish locks. There used to be a delightful song that epitomised the romantic choirboy:

His voice o'er-topped the rest,
Which was very inartistic; but the public liked it best.

However, I am not going to pretend that we were angelic!

It was not, perhaps, an easy life that we boys lived in those days. Work started at seven in the morning. Winter and summer we were aroused at 6.30 by the butler exuberantly ringing a bell up and down the long dormitory. It must have awakened not only us, but people a quarter of a mile away. But there were compensations: long and lovely walks on Sunday afternoons when, in Etons and mortar-boards, we explored the countryside; and cricket; and bathing in the stream; and Saints' Days - particularly Saints' Days, because then we had no school, and could spend our time pretty well as we liked.

And, I must add, French lessons. French used to be taught by a visiting tutor who arrived (in top-hat and frock coat) on Friday evenings. Lessons began on Fridays, and went on all Saturday morning. I am afraid we regarded them as periods of relaxation and hilarity: consequently I have never been much good at French. How that charming old French gentleman must have disliked us! I apologise to his shade.

These are but random recollections, and I could recollect for a good deal longer if I had space.

Reprinted by permission from *English Church Music*, vol. 26 (1956), pp.34-37, with the omission of purely introductory and concluding remarks.

CHAPTER 10

THE MUSIC LIBRARY

by E. H. Fellowes

Editor's Note. *This masterly survey, by one uniquely qualified to make it, was written in 1942-3. Since that time further bibliographical knowledge has modified a few of Fellowes's remarks about the rarity or the handwriting of certain items. These I have silently adjusted. His preamble is now omitted, most of its information being incorporated in the earlier chapters of the present publication; and I have also omitted a few comments which the passage of time has rendered unnecessary. For his account of the MS of Messiah I have substituted my own (not that his was fundamentally wrong) for the sake of a clearer explanation of a document not easily understood by those not intimate with Handel's methods. The subsequent disposal of the Toulouse-Philidor Collection is referred to in Chapter 8 above.*

I

The library is exceptionally rich in early and rare treatises. About 40 of these were published before the end of the 16th century and a few of them belong to the 15th. Certain of these books are not even to be found in the British Library or the Bodleian Library. This was a class of book that appealed especially to Ouseley's scholarly mind, and he was justly proud to possess so fine a collection. It is probable that he prized his treatises more than anything else in his library, with the exception of his manuscript of *Messiah*.

Only a few of these can be singled out for special mention here. Perhaps the greatest treasure consists in four volumes of the works of Franchino Gafori, namely *Theoricum opus* (Naples, 1480) and its 2nd edition under the title of *Theorica musice* (Milan, 1492), *Practica musice* (Milan, 1496), and *De harmonia musicorum instrumentorum* (Milan, 1518). Ouseley managed to secure the last three of these in early life, and for years he hoped in vain to acquire the first and rarest of the four. One of his friends eventually chanced to find it in a small bookstall in Paris and presented it to him; it was a remarkable bargain, too, at the price of about £1.[1]

Another of the incunabula in the library is the *De Arithmetica ... de Musica* of Boethius, published in 1492. A fascinating little volume is the *Liber Heroicus de Musicae laudibus* of Boemus, published in 1515. At this same date was published the *Arte de canto Llano* of Martinez de Bizcargui Gonçalo, one of only three known exemplars. Ouseley's copy of Stefano Vanneo's *Racenetum de Musica aurea* belonged formerly to de Coussemaker. *Arte del contrapunto* (1586) and *Delle imperfezioni della musica moderna* (1600) by Artusi are both first editions.

The four rare works of Petro Aron: *Compendiolo di molti dubbi* (*circa* 1545); *Luciderio in musica* (1545); *Toscanello in musica* (1529, 2nd edition); and *Trattato della natura* (1525) are all in the library. Bound up with the first of these is a tract entitled *Introduzione facilissima ... di canto fermo*, by Vincenzo Lusitano. This copy is of the 3rd edition (1561). Also bound up in this volume is *La Illuminata di tutti i tuoni di canto fermo* by Aiguino da Bressa, published in 1562. *Lilium Music*e by Michael Künspeck was first published in 1496; the copy at St Michael's is of the 5th edition (1506), but is nevertheless a rarity. The 1st edition (1537) of Sebald Heyden's *Musicae ... artis canendi*, another rarity, is interesting as one of the earliest treatises on the subject of singing. The 1st edition (1536) of the *Musurgia* of Luscinius may be mentioned, for though ten other copies survive none is in the United Kingdom. The *Dialogo* of Vincenzo Galilei, father of the famous astronomer, published in 1581, was directed against some of the theories of Guiseppe Zarlino, as set out in his *Instituzioni armoniche*; copies of both these works are at St Michael's, but that of Zarlino is of the 3rd edition (1573). The *Dodecachordon* of Glareanus is represented here in the 1st edition of 1547. The copy of Zacconi's *Prattica di musica* is of the 2nd edition (1596).

Coming to the 17th century the three volumes of the well-known *Syntagma Musicum* of Praetorius are among the most notable things in the library. The special interest of the first volume, which belongs to the 1st edition published in 1615, lies in the fact that it contains the following endorsement on the title-page: 'J.B.Bach alumnus Schole Thom

1720 E 1 Jan.' The year is slightly conjectural because it was subsequently written over to convert it to 1739, and at the same time the initial B was changed into an E. The words 'alumnus Schole Thom' were evidently inserted later in the narrow space below the name and above the date. The 'E' stands for 'Era' and is similar to A.D., as denoting the mèthod of reckoning time. [J.B.Bach (1676-1749) was 1st cousin to Johann Sebastian Bach, and he was the father of J.E.Bach (1722-77) who was briefly a pupil of his older cousin once removed (Johann Sebastian) at St Thomas's School, Leipzig. - Editor.] The second and third volumes, bound together in their original vellum covers, contain the signature of G.P.Telemann dated 1712.

Other rare 17th-century works highly valued by Ouseley are *Il compendio della musica* by Orazio Tigrini (1602, 2nd edition); *Regole di musica* by Giovanni d'Avella (1657); and the Spanish treatise of Cerone entitled *El Melopeo* (1613) which had once belonged to Crotch, one of his predecessors in the Oxford chair of music. Passing over the works of Doni, Donfridi, Gumpeltzhaimer, de Caux, Francisco Correa de Arauxo, and several others at St Michael's, notable examples from the latter part of the 17th century are *Sistema Musico* by Lemme Rossi (1666), *Documenti armonici* (1687), and *Il perchè Musicale* (1693), both by Angelo Berardi.

Among the very numerous theoretical publications of the 18th and 19th centuries of which there are copies at Tenbury are such standard works as those of Heinichen, Marpurg, Mattheson, Telemann, Quantz, and Türk. Early English musical treatises in the library include the 1st edition of Thomas Morley's *A Plaine and Easie Introduction to Practicall Musicke* (1597), Dowland's *Ornithoparcus* (1609), Matthew Locke's *Melothesia* (1673), Christopher Sympson's *Compendium of practicall Musick* (1667), and John Playford's *Introduction to the Skill of Musick* (1660).

Though it cannot strictly be classed as a theoretical treatise, mention may be made of John Case's *The Praise of Musicke* (1588), which is a rare book. Byrd wrote a motet for six voices as 'A gratification unto Master John Case for his learned booke, lately made in praise of Musicke'.

Apart from valuable books of this character there are some hundreds of volumes in the library at St Michael's dealing with almost every kind of subject connected with music down to modern times.

II

There is a very large amount of printed music at St Michael's, including almost all the English church music of any standing, down to the 20th century. Secular vocal music is also well represented; and there are a good many scores of orchestral works and chamber music, pianoforte music, organ music, oratorios, and songs, while the collection of operatic scores is unusually large and important.

Among the earliest printed music books in this library is a very fine large folio containing Masses for Five Voices by Orlando di Lasso. This was published at Milan by Adam Berg in 1574. It is one of those large choir books of the kind that when set open on a stand enabled several singers to read their various parts from a single copy; the voice parts were printed independently on each page, not in score, and in such large type that the music could easily be seen several feet away. There is a similar volume of Masses for Five Voices, also by this same composer, which was published in 1589. Inside the cover of this book there has been pasted a single sheet index of its contents in manuscript; a statement in an 18th-century hand is endorsed on this page to the effect that it is in the handwriting of Orlando di Lasso. The library also has a third volume of the same size and character; this was published in 1589, and it contains Masses for Five and Six Voices by Francisco Sale, a Belgian composer.

Among the sets of printed quarto partbooks is the collection of *Cantiones Sacrae* for four, five, six, and eight voices of Orlando di Lasso, published in 1582. The earliest of all these sets in the St Michael's library is a unique copy of the First Book of Motets for Five Voices by

Giovanni Animuccia, published in 1552. There are two sets of *Cantiones Sacrae* by Friedrich Linder (1586 and 1590). Claude le Jeune's set of Psalms, published in 1589, is another interesting work of which the complete parts are in the library. Among the printed editions of Italian madrigals are the works of Luca Marenzio, who is represented here by the complete partbooks of his 1st, 3rd, 4th, 5th, and 6th books of Madrigals for Six Voices, mostly in their 1st edition. There are also three of the madrigal sets of Pomponio Nenna. Other works by foreign composers of this character on the same shelves are the Psalms of Giovanni Legrenzi and of G.B.Bassani.

The Elizabethan and Jacobean composers are fairly well represented at Tenbury, considering the great rarity of the madrigalian partbooks and the song books of the Lutenists. Morley's *Canzonets to three Voyces* (1593) is a somewhat rare exemplar. The 2nd edition (1600) of his *Madrigalls to Foure Voyces* is also here. There is a fine copy of the complete partbooks of Byrd's First Set of *Cantiones sacrae* (1589) and also of his *Songs of sundrie natures* of the same date. Another rarity is Sir William Leighton's *Teares or Lamentacions of a Sorrowfull Soule* (1614); and a copy of Amner's *Sacred Hymnes* (1615) is also on these shelves.

The Tenbury copy of Dowland's *First Booke of Songs or Ayres* was published in 1613. This is the 4th edition, but it is extremely rare. Dowland's *Second Book* is also in this library; this is the 1st edition of 1600. The last line of the words is missing in the song 'White as Lilies' in all the printed copies of this book known to the writer; it has fortunately been recovered, having been added in manuscript by a contemporary hand in the Tenbury copy. The Tenbury copy of *Parthenia*, the famous collection of keyboard works by Byrd, Bull, and Gibbons, is a unique survivor of an edition of 1646. The original edition was issued in 1611 and the existence of this 1646 edition long remained entirely unknown to bibliographers. It contains some distinctive features which have been duly noted in it.

Complete copies of *Musica Deo Sacra* by Thomas Tomkins, published in 1668, some twelve years after his death, are extremely rare. The four partbooks and the *Pars organica* are complete at St Michael's, but the organ part is unique, because at the end of the book details are printed which are found in no other copy, indicating precisely the pitch prevailing in Tomkins's experience. The Tenbury copy provides the only known precise evidence in this matter, and it establishes the fact that the customary pitch for church music in England in Elizabethan and Jacobean times, as indicated by the notation, was practically a minor third higher than that in use today.

No more than passing mention can be made here of copies of the two volumes of *Orpheus Britannicus* (1st edition, 1698-1702); of *Amphion Anglicus* (1700); of John Playford's *Psalms and Hymns* (1st edition of 1671) recently presented by Mr Maurice Bevan; and the second book, 1693, with *Two Divine Hymns* (1700); of Blow's *Ode on the death of Purcell* (1696), and the *Choice Psalms* of Henry and William Lawes (1648). A copy of the original edition of Purcell's Te Deum and Jubilate in D is also on these shelves.

Few libraries can be so richly furnished with the scores of French and Italian opera from the end of the 17th century until the middle of the 19th as is that of St Michael's. The manuscripts will be dealt with presently, but something must be said here of the remarkable collection of about 250 printed volumes, handsomely bound at the period in uniform style, and issued by French publishers in the late 18th and early 19th centuries. These volumes include full scores of operas by such composers as Auber, Berton, Boieldieu, Dalayrac, Gluck, Grétry, N. de M. Isouard, Kreutzer, Mehul, Piccini, and Rossini among others. There are also a number of scores giving pianoforte accompaniment to the same works in place of full score. Among the publishers of these are Janet et Cotelle, J. Frey, and Imbault. Each volume is numbered on the back with a small paper label, and it is clear from these numbers that at one time the collection was even larger.

How this fine collection came into Sir Frederick's possession is not known, but it is more than likely that it was bought by his father, for a considerable purchase of music books was made by Sir Gore in Paris, the conveyance of which to England offered some difficulty. The following letter, preserved among Miss Ouseley's collection of autographs (see above, p.66), may well refer to these volumes, although unfortunately the date of the year is not given.

> My dear Sir Gore
> If the music you wish to have from Paris is divided in small parcels and properly addressed to me, let it be sent to Baron Werther's the Prussian Minister's at Paris, who will find the means to forward it to me by weekly English and French Messengers. It gives me great pleasure to be able to meet your wish.
> ever sincerely yours
> Bülow
>
> Gt. Cumberland Place
> July the 12th.

The rare printed series of operas and motets of the period of Louis XIV that are included in the Toulouse Collection (not to be confused with the collection just mentioned) are inseparable from the Philidor manuscripts for the purpose of discussion; they will be dealt with presently.

The library is well supplied in various editions with full scores of the operas and masses of Mozart. Printed scores of the operas of Gluck and Rossini, and of Beethoven's *Fidelio*, among many other standard works, are also here.

III

Among the manuscripts pride of place must be given to the score of *Messiah* (MSS 346-7). This is not the original manuscript of the work, which is now in the British Library. To appreciate the significance of the manuscript belonging to St Michael's it is necessary to understand Handel's methods of work in his maturity. When he had finished writing a work he caused a neat copy to be made by a copyist, J.C.Smith, for his personal use when directing performances. The St Michael's manuscript is such a copy, made immediately upon completion of composition, and forming what is known as a 'conducting' score. So it was that it was this manuscript which Handel used at the first performance of the oratorio in Dublin in 1742, and at all subsequent performances under his own direction. And it was into this copy that he entered the names of the singers who were to perform the various solos in those performances. Moreover, when he came to revise, or even to re-write, certain movements, these altered forms were interleaved into this copy, not the original manuscript. For the history of the work after its initial composition, and for certain very important revisions the manuscript owned by Ouseley is therefore of prime importance even though in its origin it was no more than a fair copy in another hand. The re-written movements found here, but not in the original manuscript, are 'But who may abide the day of his coming?', 'Rejoice greatly', 'Their sound is gone out', 'Why do the nations?', and 'Thou art gone up on high'. The manuscript had much hard wear and was subject to much alteration in Handel's lifetime, so that at the end of his life it was necessary to write it out anew, and that copy is now in Hamburg. The St Michael's copy came on the market in 1838, when it was bought by E.J.Ottley, one of the original Fellows of St Michael's College, who presented it to Sir Frederick Ouseley in 1867.[2]

There are in the library several other volumes of Handel's works copied by J.C.Smith or those associated with him, including certain of the 'Chandos' anthems (MSS 881-83). Here too is a score of his opera *Amadis* (MS 884), marked on the back with a label 'G.F.H.', while inside there is a press-mark, probably marking its position on some library shelves. A transcript by Smith of *Acis and Galatea* (MS 885) was another of Ottley's presents to Ouseley.

Apart from the Handelian manuscripts there are in the library three main groups of important manuscripts, namely those dealing with (1) the Polyphonic school, both English and Italian; (2) with the Restoration school, and particularly with the works of Purcell and Blow; (3) with opera.

(1) The library is exceptionally rich in early text of polyphonic church music. Ouseley owned as many as ten sets of partbooks, amounting to 50 books in all, dating approximately from the year 1600 (MSS 341-4. 349-89. 807-11). The text contained in these partbooks is of first rate importance to musical scholarship, especially as many compositions are to be found there and not elsewhere. Among such English works are Taverner's motet *Sospitati dedit*, Byrd's *Circumspice Jerusalem* and *Petrus beatus*, Kirbye's *Vox in Rama* and portions of an otherwise unknown Mass for Seven Voices by Tallis. In addition to these is a single partbook (MS 389), apparently the sole survivor of a set, bearing on the top margins the intials 'W B', which it is tempting to think might be those of William Byrd. The paper used is that sold by Thomas East under whose monopoly the ruled music paper was issued.[3]

Another manuscript of the same period (MS 340) includes a large number of motets adapted for solo performance on the lute - much as favourite choruses from oratorios were adapted for the pianoforte in the 19th century. It is a beautiful example of penmanship in lute tablature. A lovely example of penmanship in ordinary notation is to be seen in the manuscript of Thomas Hunt's Four-part Service (MS 786). This was rescued from a bundle of rubbish in 1919. It also is written on East's ruled paper and marked 'T E'. No other text of this service is known.

Two manuscript sets of partbooks (MSS 940-44 and 1162-7) contain very large collections of madrigals. Most of these are Italian, but they also include a few English examples that are not to be found in the contemporary printed sets, though they belong to the great madrigalian period. These two collections were owned by James Bartleman, a notable bass singer, who formed a valuable musical library dispersed after his death in 1821.

Of outstanding importance in this group is the famous organ-book (MS 791) which has come to be associated with the name of Adrian Batten, and is perhaps to be accounted the most valuable book in the St Michael's library from the point of view of musicology. Completed in 1638, it consists of nearly 500 folios and it includes 256 pieces of English church music, a very large proportion of which are otherwise unknown. Among the special rarities it includes the whole of Byrd's Great Service and as many as five Services by Weelkes that have not otherwise survived. As in other organ books of the period the music is written in short score on two staves of six lines each, and unfortunately the inner vocal parts, also in accordance with the custom of the time, are usually only lightly sketched, and sometimes no more than the treble and bass parts are shown. Yet this manuscript is indispensable for the reconstruction of many of the finest 'Tudor' services and anthems.

A few important early manuscript partbooks have been added quite recently to the library. Among these is a set of three partbooks (MSS 1469-71), the survivors of a set of five, which were bought from the library of Sir Leicester Harmsworth after his death in 1937. They are in their original covers and may be dated *circa* 1600. They are in the same hand as MSS 354-8. Another recent acquisition is an extremely fine single bass partbook (MS 1464); it may be considered the finest partbook in the library. The music is written in a very bold hand dating from *circa* 1575. It contains an unusually large number of compositions, including examples of Fairfax, Taverner, Tallis, and Robert Johnson, and some of the text is unique.

MS 1486 was bought in 1942. It was formerly in the Braikenridge Art Collection at Brislington near Bristol. It is a beautiful manuscript in the hand of John Sadler and dated 1591. It is decorated with grotesques and fine initial letters and the script is of particular beauty. It is a single tenor partbook supplying text of motets by Taverner, Tallis, and White hitherto unknown. The contratenor book of the same set is owned by Captain R.Y.Berkeley of Spetchley Park, Worcester; that belonged formerly to Miss Willmott of Great Warley.

(2) Passing to the Restoration period, the library includes much contemporary text of authoritative importance, especially in relation to the works of Purcell and Blow.

Among Purcell's early works, the Tenbury score of *Dido and Aeneas*, which is an early 18th-century manuscript (MS 1266), is regarded as the most authentic text of this opera. It is here entitled *The loves of Aeneas and Dido*. A complete set of the separate vocal and instrumental parts of Purcell's *Ode for St Cecilia's Day*, 1692 (MS 1309) may be dated about the year 1700. The anthem *O Lord, rebuke me not* as found in MS 789 and attributed there to Purcell has all the appearance of being genuine though not otherwise known. If the three anthems in MS 1227b, *O Lord, thou art my God*; *The Lord is King*; and *The Lord, even the most mighty God* are rightly there attributed to Purcell, this is the unique source of their text.

Daniel Purcell is well represented at St Michael's in contemporary text. His Ode written in 1696 for the installation of the Duke of Gloucester as a Knight of the Garter at the age of seven is wrongly described in MS 1175 as 'The Duke of Gloucester's Birthday Ode' by Henry Purcell. It is an entirely different work both as regards words and music. This same manuscript also includes 15 of Purcell's anthems stated to be 'transcribed from the original source in 1680 in the handwriting of the author'

A large number of anthems by John Blow are among the Tenbury manuscripts. One of the most important manuscripts of this period consists of a splendid folio set of choir partbooks, together with three volumes containing the same works in organ score, all in the hand of John Gostling (MSS 1176-82). There is also a smaller collection of similar character copied by Gostling (MSS 797-803), and both contain large quantities of Blow's church music and also many compositions by his contemporaries. The full score of Blow's anthem *God spake sometime in visions* (MS 1008), written for the coronation of James II, is in the composer's hand.

No more than passing mention can be made here of the many compositions found among the Tenbury manuscripts of

Humfrey, Croft, Jeremiah Clarke, Michael Wise, and several others of the same school. It is necessary also to pass over the works of a number of notable foreign composers of this same period, of which much manuscript text is in this library.

The ode is a type of secular composition which is characteristic of English music of this period when it first originated. It extends through the 18th-century, and it cannot be left quite unnoticed here, seeing that it is well represented in the St Michael's manuscripts. Besides works by Purcell and Blow there are also scores (some of them autograph) by Croft (MSS 1221, 1231) and Jeremiah Clarke (1232); and at a later date similar works by William and Philip Hayes (1261-65). The score of Charles Burney's *Ode to Fancy* (MS 1212) is another interesting autograph in this class of composition. The character and form of the musical ode was somewhat changed in the 19th century, but examples of such works are among these manuscripts; for instance, an ode by Stafford Smith (MS 1322) and two odes by Ouseley himself (MS 1191).

(3) The subject of the third group is opera. The fine comprehensive set of printed scores of such works, published mostly in Paris, has already been mentioned in reference to the printed music. There is also in the library a very large number of complete scores of operas of the 18th- and 19th-century composers in contemporary manuscripts, as well as many more volumes of operatic selections. These are all in addition to the splendid Toulouse-Philidor Collection, which must be described separately. There are nearly 200 of these volumes, 92 of which are occupied with the full scores of as many as 46 operas; several of them have never been published. Among them are as many as 19 full scores of operas by Paisiello and seven by Rossini. Other composers represented in these volumes are Bianchi, Donizetti, Mayer, Bellini, Cimarosa, Jommelli, Mercadante, and Prati. The manuscript full score of Galuppi's *Siröe* in three volumes (MSS 1060-62) belonged formerly to 'Prince Charlie' (the Young Pretender). A full manuscript score of Spohr's

Jessonda in three volumes is also on these shelves (MSS 1100-1102).

The now famous Toulouse-Philidor Collection has been fully described in *Music & Letters*, vol.21 (1931), pp.116-129. It is certainly one of the greatest, if not the greatest, feature of the St Michael's library. It consists of over 400 volumes bound uniformly in their original calf binding, stamped on both covers with the coat-of-arms of the comte de Toulouse surmounting two anchors to denote his rank as Admiral of France.

This collection was put together in the first place for the use of the Count, who was a son of Louis XIV and Madame de Montespan, at his palace at Rambouillet. It includes about 350 volumes of manuscript, almost all of which are in the hand of André Philidor, music librarian to Louis XIV at Versailles, and of his eldest son. These are supplemented by about 70 printed volumes, so that, for example, the operas of Lully are completely represented, chiefly by manuscript scores and for the rest by very rare printed scores. There are also some volumes of motets and other church music. Besides the full scores in fine folio volumes containing the operas and ballets of Lully and the operas of Campra, Colasse, Desmarets, Destouches, Marais, and others, there are the corresponding sets of single partbooks, both of the voice parts and the instrumental parts of these same works, almost all of which are inscribed 'copiez par l'order de son Altesse Serenissime le comte de Toulouze par Philidor l'ainé ... et par son fils aîné'.

Apart from the folio scores both printed and manuscript there are about 30 oblong quarto volumes containing the printed scores of French opera of the same period. Besides the composers already mentioned, these include works of Theobaldo de Gatti, J.B.Stuck, J.Bertin, L.J.Bourgeois, J.J.Mouret, M.Lacoste, and M.Royer among others.

The whole collection passed by inheritance from Toulouse to his son, the Duke of Penthièvre, then to his grand-daughter, who married the Duke of Orleans, and so to their son, King Louis-Philippe. It was then that the books came to the Palais Royal in Paris, and were stamped 'Bibliothèque du Roi'. After the death of Louis-Philippe the whole library was dispersed in a Paris sale-room in 1852. The greater part of this collection of music, comprising about 290 volumes of manuscript and 67 printed volumes, was bought by a man named Williams-Hope, a rather eccentric Englishman then living in Paris. All these volumes were shortly afterwards acquired by Sir Frederick Ouseley, who seems not to have known their history further back than when they were at the Palais Royal in the time of Louis-Philippe. The remainder of the collection, consisting chiefly of motets with their corresponding partbooks, and including also some further works of Lully, was bought at the sale in 1852 by a Frenchman named Crétain.

By an amazing chance Crétain's purchase, numbering 60 volumes, was never split up; it appeared in its entirety in 1935 in the hands of an English book dealer in Paris named Arthur Rau. St Michael's College not having at the moment the ready funds to purchase these volumes, money was generously made available for the purpose by Canon G.C.E.Ryley so that they could safely be secured and reunited with the rest of the Toulouse Collection. Within a few months it was possible to repay Canon Ryley's advance from disposal balances. It is noteworthy that by some error at the sale of 1852 the set of ten volumes of Lalande's motets had been split up between Williams-Hope and Crétain. These were now once more united.[4]

There are five more books at Tenbury in the hand of Philidor which are not part of the Toulouse Collection. These are service books from the Chapel Royal of Louis XIV. They are stamped on their handsome morocco binding with the Royal Arms of France. The five volumes were bought by Ouseley in 1849 at the London rooms of Messrs Puttick and Simpson.

The manuscript of an opera, *Comala, Azion Teatrale* by Pietro Morandi, in two volumes (MSS 849-50), is in its original calf binding, but the arms stamped on the covers are not those of the half-brother of the comte de Toulouse as formerly stated but of King Ferdinand I of the Two Sicilies.

In conclusion a few miscellaneous manuscripts may be mentioned as being of special interest. MS 348 contains the recitatives and choruses from the opera *Orione* by J.C.Bach. It is stated there that the original score having been destroyed by fire at the Opera House, no other copy was believed to exist. A collection of 81 organ pieces, dated 1792, is in the hand of Gottfried Bach (MS 301). Ouseley endorsed MS 510, which contains church music by Gaetano Carpani, as follows: 'Many of these compositions are in Carpani's hand and are probably unique.' An early 18th-century setting of the St Matthew Passion, by C.F.Rollen (MS 898), is perhaps in the composer's hand; this is a very early example of a setting of the Passion in this elaborate form. Two volumes of church music by Pachelbel (MSS 1208-9) may well be in his autograph; these belonged to William Boyce. A Magnificat with full orchestra by this same composer constitutes MS 1356.

A setting of *Domine ad adiuvandum* by Colonna is another possible autograph, which at one time belonged to Charles Wesley (MS 932). A treatise entitled *Musico Pratico* by Bononcini is considered probably to be the author's original manuscript (MS 967); it was published in Bologna in 1678. Christopher Sympson's instrumental work entitled *The Seasons* may be in the composer's writing, and the manuscript of his *Compendium of Practicall Musick* (MS 390) has the appearance of being the copy used by the printer when the work was published in 1667.

Among more recent manuscripts is that of Stainer's well-known anthem *I saw the Lord* (MS 1352). Another interesting item is the full score of Spohr's symphony *Die Jahrzeitung*, which is in the composer's handwriting. It is to be regretted that some of the autographs mentioned in the earliest editions of *Grove's Dictionary of Music and Musicians* cannot now be found. Among these were stated to be examples of Mozart, Paganini, and Mendelssohn.

Naturally, a very large number of Ouseley's manuscripts in his own hand have an honoured place on these shelves. These include examples of his early experiments as a very young child, most of which are in the hand of his mother or sister (MSS 660, 1146, 1370-73). One of his childish experiments in opera, entitled *Tom and his Mamma* (MS 1087) is dated 1832. A collection of 18 of his early instrumental compositions (MS 759), dated 1839, includes five violoncello sonatas, which, as he is known to have played the cello, he perhaps wrote for himself. Among his many mature works, both instrumental and vocal, the following scores in his own hand may be mentioned: a Service for Holy Communion for double choir and full orchestra (MS 1192); Te Deum and Benedictus for 8-part chorus and solo voices with accompaniments for full orchestra and organ (MS 1186); several cathedral Services (MSS 841-2, 1358-60, and among other collections); nine anthems for voices, orchestra, and organ (MS 1187); and many other anthems scattered among various bound volumes.

There is a full score of his oratorio *Hagar* (MS 331), but no more than the chorus parts of *St Polycarp* (MSS 945-54) are now to be found among Ouseley's manuscripts. But there are two autograph scores of his sacred cantata *The Lord is the true God* (MSS 992 and 1190 [the latter now in the Faculty of Music library at Oxford - Editor]. In addition to these there are numbers of glees and partsongs (MSS 959, 1154, 1219); songs (1145); overtures and other orchestral works (332, 1189, 1374-77); and organ solos (1369).

Nor must the many manuscript scores of 16th- and 17th-century music made by Sir Frederick be overlooked. Conspicuous among these is a set of eight partbooks (MSS 590-97) containing as many as 172 motets of the continental polyphonic school, among which are 65 works of Palestrina. Another notable volume (MS 1033; see p.52 above) is described as containing 'Ancient Cathedral Services collected from various sources and carefully revised by F.A.G.Ouseley'. These, and many more, form a worthy record of his untiring industry, his fine scholarship, and his beautiful musical penmanship.

Reprinted by permission from *The History of St Michael's College, Tenbury*, edited by M.F.Alderson and H.C.Colles (London, SPCK, 1943), pp.78-101, with slight revisions.

EDITORIAL POSTSCRIPT. Under the Trust Deed for the College dated 1864 some part of Sir Frederick Ouseley's Music Library was vested absolutely in the Trust. Under his will the other part became trust property subject to an eventual gift to the Bodleian Library, Oxford, should it become necessary to sell or break up the General Library of the College. Unfortunately there was no means of knowing the exact demarcation between the two parts. When, following the closure of the College, sale of the General Library became imminent, an amicable settlement was agreed with the Bodleian Library and approved by the Charity Commission whereby all the music manuscripts passed to that Library, while all the printed music and books on music remained trust property, with the proviso that the Bodleian Library might purchase such of the printed music and books on music which it did not already possess at an agreed valuation rather than at any public sale by auction which might take place. A small group of manuscripts acquired since Sir Frederick Ouseley's death has been placed on deposit in the Bodleian Library.

CHAPTER 11

THE BUILDINGS

by Charles A. Nicholson

The interest of Sir Charles Nicholson, who was by profession an architect, was aroused through his younger brother, Sir Sydney Nicholson, a Fellow of St Michael's College. His redundant references to portraits (now more fully and precisely dealt with in Appendix K) are omitted, and where he confusingly speaks of the church under the heading of the college this has been adjusted. Many other details may be found in four articles by J.S.Bumpus on 'The Architecture of St Michael's Church and College' in The Architect and Contract Reporter *for 3, 10, 17, 24 July 1903.*

The architect of St Michael's Church and College was Henry Woodyer, a pupil of Butterfield, and the buildings have undergone no material alteration since they were completed in 1856-7, a fact which testifies to the excellence of their general arrangement and construction.

The general layout is good and the buildings look well from all sides; the architectural details are consistent and of considerable refinement.

Woodyer never experimented in audacious colour schemes, but in many respects his work was obviously inspired by that of his master, Butterfield. A great deal of it was done in Surrey and Hampshire, the parish church at Dorking [of later date than St Michael's] being a very noteworthy building. In the course of his career he did a good deal of domestic work which it is interesting to compare with that done by Butterfield. Both master and pupil obviously paid close attention to detail, but the master's outlook was far more modern and progressive than that of the pupil. The buildings at Tenbury are contemporary with Street's theological college at Cuddesdon, and the two buildings are very much alike in detail, but Street's college is not so well planned as Woodyer's, nor are its architectural merits greater. Evidently at Tenbury there was no stint of money; dignity was demanded, luxury was despised. So the architect's opportunity must have been an ideal one and Woodyer rose to the occasion.

The general disposition of the buildings is quite simple: the church stands on the north side of the site next to the high road; the college buildings are concentrated in a single block to the south of the church, and the Warden's lodging, backed with a timber cloister connecting the college buildings with the church, forms the east side of a three-sided quadrangle open to the west. The site falls steeply from the north-east to south-west and full advantage has been taken of this. The buildings are undeniably pictorial, although they are pronounced examples of a school of architecture with which present-day critics are not in sympathy. The details are on the whole good and carefully thought out but give the impression that the architect aimed at producing a collection of reproductions of 13th- and 14th-century ornament; a genuine mediæval building would have been much simpler.

It was never, of course, intended that the result should be mistaken for anything other than a 19th-century building: the gothic revival architects did not attempt such follies, though their enemies accused them of doing so. But they did hope to recapture some of the spirit of the mediæval builders, and in this, it must be confessed, Woodyer was only successful to a very limited extent, though he took great pains to do his work in a consistent manner, reviving traditional methods of construction as well as mediæval principles of design and ornament. Probably, however, he as nearly hit the mark as many of his contemporaries.

He must have been in complete sympathy with his employer; his architecture seems the exact counterpart of the Founder's ideas concerning church music and ceremonial.

The church, which is the dominant feature of the group, though not on a large scale, is very successful in expressing the fact that it is something more than a mere parish church. Moreover, it looks a good deal larger than it is and does not look like a small copy of a large church. In attaining these results Woodyer succeeded where many others have failed.

The building is cruciform and the chancel has an apse. Nave, chancel, and transepts are of equal height and have very steep roofs ceiled with timber vaulting, which in the nave and chancel is unbroken from east to west, the transept vaultings being treated independently, a very clever device for obtaining an effect of considerable length. The architectural detail is based upon English 14th-century work of a somewhat florid type but quite refined and shapely. Both the masonry and the structural woodwork are very good and solid, but the arches between the nave and aisles, which are carried on thin columns of blue Penmant stone with heavy capitals carved with decadent foliage, detract from the effect of an otherwise very dignified interior.

Externally the church looks exotic and rather pretentious, but it is not fair to criticize it as an isolated building; it should be regarded as a part of a group of buildings designed to fulfil very exceptional requirements.

The arrangements and fittings of the church are very interesting. Some of the carving is quite good. The glass in the apse is exceptionally fine: it is by Hardman, and recalls that in the apse of St Chad's Cathedral at Birmingham, presumably designed by Pugin. The rest of the glass is tolerably good and there are some scraps of old glass in the windows of a small passage round the south transept. This transept is filled up with the organ and the north transept forms a baptistery, with the font in the centre under a very tall cover. There is a well in the corner of the baptistery and the chapel to the east of this transept has been furnished in recent years.

The arrangements of the sanctuary are of quite unusual dignity and are more generous than those considered adequate in many of our cathedrals.

There are no seats east of the transepts; the steps are exceptionally well arranged and there are not too many of them. There are canopied sedilia on the epistle side but no piscina, and the credence, strange to say, is on the gospel side of the altar. This is of good proportions, and stands forward in the apse under a not very successful canopied reredos. The sanctuary is paved with mosaics and the chancel with encaustic tiles, simpler tile paving being used in the nave.

The choir seats are in line with the transepts. There are 14 stalls with carved misericords. Front desks for the boys have been added in recent years. There are no return stalls, but the chancel is enclosed with very good and simple iron screens; the western one was originally adorned with a row of seven candlesticks. The pulpit is a commonplace stone one. The nave is seated with very unworthy pews of pitch pine, and the heating and lighting arrangements are modern. The chancel was originally lighted with candles fixed on the choir desks and there were hanging coronæ of lamps and candles elsewhere.

In some practical details Woodyer's work is open to criticism. Here, for instance, there is no convenient access to the greater part of the roofs for the purpose of repair. Such an omission was seldom made by Woodyer's master, Butterfield. The only piece of roof at Tenbury which possesses a parapet is that of the apse; elsewhere very long and heavy ladders must be required for all repair work.

Again, the access originally provided to the great dormitory was very inadequate. But if Woodyer was sometimes forgetful he was upon the whole a sound constructor and his buildings have stood the test of time very well.

From a purely architectural point of view the secular portions of the buildings are more successful than the church. Although they can obviously be criticised as foreign looking and over-ornate it cannot fairly be denied that the work is finely proportioned and consistently carried out. The main block has a long cloister facing north, with a series of rooms opening from it facing south; the library at the east end and the hall at the west end with smaller rooms and a mezzanine between them. Near the hall is a wing projecting northwards containing offices, and at the end of the building the fall of the ground enabled the architect to plan a roomy and airy basement storey.

The great dormitory is formed in the roof of the main block and there is a smaller dormitory, known as the 'chapel dormitory', in the roof above the north-west wing. The Founder is said to have provided this room to serve as a domestic chapel in the event of any trouble arising with the ecclesiastical authorities, but happily he was left in peace at Tenbury to do his own work in his own way.

The Warden's house on the east side of the three-sided courtyard is sensibly designed with well lighted, comfortable rooms, and the timber cloister against the west side of the Warden's house is quite an attractive piece of craftsmanship.

All the interior of the domestic buildings is treated consistently, not, as one often sees in domestic gothic buildings of the period, with conventional jerry-builders' internal finishings. Here the ceiling joints are exposed, the doors and fireplaces simply and naturally treated, such details as the door hinges carefully and well designed.

The library is a fine room, though rather dark, and so lofty that the upper bookshelves are difficult of access; there is no gallery. The dining hall is a very beautiful room, not very large but lofty in proportion, well lighted and panelled and furnished in oak. There is a picturesque minstrel's gallery over the screened entrance lobby and there used to be a canopied fireplace before the present central heating was put in. [In 1968 the entrance lobby was thrown into the hall to enlarge the dining accommodation. - Editor.]

In sum, then, these buildings are of very considerable interest, both as fine architecture and as a very favourable expression of the artistic ideas of a bygone generation of great men.

Reprinted by permission from *The History of St Michael's College, Tenbury*, edited by M.F.Alderson and H.C.Colles (London, SPCK, 1943),pp.124-9.

VALEDICTION

by the Archbishop of Canterbury

Lambeth Palace, SE1 7JU

MESSAGE FOR THE SERVICE OF THANKSGIVING AT ST MICHAEL'S, TENBURY - 14 July 1985

My thoughts are with you as you prepare to hold your Service of Thanksgiving for the work and witness of St Michael's College over more than a century and a quarter.

With its magnificent library, the catalogue of distinguished musicians who have been members of its staff, and its illustrious list of Old Boys, St Michael's needs no help from me to secure its reputation. Thanks to the College, the standard of cathedral music is higher today than it has ever been.

Though I shall be sharing your sadness that this happy and triumphant chapter in the history of the English Church and its music is drawing to a close, I shall also be thanking God for all that has been achieved since St Michael's was founded.

The College has completed its task. But the spirit of Tenbury will live on through all those who learned to love their Church and its music at St Michael's.

+Robert Cantuar:

St Michael's College, Tenbury
c/o The Reverend Andrew Walters

APPENDICES

APPENDIX A
The 'Charles II' Bible and Prayer Book
(see p.3)

The survival in Sir Frederick Ouseley's possession of the strikingly handsome Bible and Prayer Book bearing the bookplate of his maternal grandfather, John Whitelock, and carrying on their covers the cypher of Charles II, raises a tantalising question. What can have been the provenance of such treasures?

John Whitelocke is unlikely to have acquired them for bibliographical reasons. Ouseley did not put them on the library shelves at St Michael's College, but kept them apart in a metal box or trunk. These indications point to the idea of a family possession. The only connection with the time of Charles II that might account for it lies in Sir Bulstrode Whitelocke. But in view of his prominence as a statesman under Cromwell (Ambassador to Sweden, and several times Commissioner of the Great Seal) is it likely that something so closely connected with Charles II would have come into his hands?

He did, as a matter of fact, perform a service of some value to Charles II (and to scholarship). During the Commonwealth he used his position to save certain books and manuscripts (one of them no less than the *Codex Alexandrinus*) which would otherwise have been plundered. He was fortunate enough to be included in the pardons granted after the Restoration, and through an intermediary he managed to obtain an audience of the king. At this he took the opportunity to return the royal volumes and to present some of his own. Did he then receive this Bible and Prayer Book as a mark of royal appreciation? Though his own diary, which contains an account of this interview, says nothing about any present from the king to himself, R. H. Whitelocke, writing in 1860 in his ***Memoirs** Biographical and Historical of Bulstrode **Whitelocke***, reports that the king made him a gift of a 'coronation' Bible and Prayer Book. However, Bulstrode Whitelocke's interview with the king was held in mid June 1660, while the coronation did not take place until April 1661. Still, by the 19th century the expression 'coronation Bible' might easily be an innocent transformation of 'a magnificent royal Bible', or something of the sort. At the same time one cannot but reflect that, as the king did not return to London until 29 May 1660, there must have been some quick work if the bindings were ready by the middle of June.

Though one's inclination is to accept that these books represent an inheritance from Sir Bulstrode Whitelocke (and, if so, tend to support Sir Frederick Ouseley's descent from him), the matter remains less than conclusive. R. H. Whitelocke did not know that the books survived at the date he wrote, and he was unaware of any Ouseley family connection. For reliable information about Whitelocke's audience with the king, see Ruth Spalding, *The Reluctant*

Puritan (London, Faber & Faber, 1975), pp.228-9. E. H. Fellowes was under a misapprehension in saying (A&C, p.79) that Sir Frederick Ouseley's mother was 'the last representative and heiress of the Whitelocke family', for Dr Spalding mentions various later members of it. The error is also found in *The Tenbury Letters*, edited by E.H.Fellowes and Edward Pine (London, Golden Cockerel Press, 1942), p.6.

When Fellowes began work on cataloguing the Music Library at St Michael's College in 1918 he came across the box containing these treasures, by that time reposing unrecognised hitherto 'in a cupboard together with some tin cans and other lumber'. It was through him that they came to be sold to Queen Mary.

APPENDIX B
Sir Gore Ouseley's Presentation Gold Plate
(see p.4)

The gold plate presented to Sir Gore Ouseley by the Shah was in Sir Frederick Ouseley's possession at the time of his death. Very shortly thereafter, yielding to persuasion on grounds of family sentiment, the College trustees with innocent guilelessness unwarily allowed it to be held for life in turn by two distant Ouseley connections under covenant for its eventual return. When, on the death of the second of these, it was duly claimed, it was stated to have been lost and the College was able to obtain only modest financial recompense. That was in 1907.

Nothing more was known about it by the College until the appearance of a brochure, *The Palace Collections of Egypt*, prepared by Messrs Sotheby in connection with the sale by auction in Cairo of the property of ex-King Farouk of Egypt in February and March 1954 by order of the Egyptian government. A photograph of it with accompanying caption in this brochure constituted clear and authentic identification. The brochure also revealed that, quite unknown to the College, the plate had been exhibited at Burlington House in 1931. A valiant attempt by Mr F. S. Miles, the College legal adviser, to assert ownership in 1954 failed on account of lapse of time. At the sale it failed to raise £5,000 and was withdrawn. Its present ownership is unknown. Apparently it was of English, not Persian manufacture.

APPENDIX C

Abstract of Sir Henry Bishop's Report on Ouseley's Exercise for the B Mus degree (Ouseley MS 10)

(see p.14)

Bishop expresses his general standpoint thus: 'Whatever you may do in any other work may be regulated by your own taste and opinion; but in my judgment of your "Exercise" I conceive I am bound by orthodox principles.' Most of his observations refer to minor infractions of grammatical principles, but far more interesting are his numerous observations on instrumentation, in which, as an experienced conductor and composer, he was much more expert than young Ouseley could hope to be. Thus, for example:

> I do not like the Dominant Pedal being employed as you have written in the horn parts - the harshness is too great.
>
> I would always avoid high notes for the Alto Trombone.
>
> I would remark that very high notes for the Clarionet should be avoided.
>
> The A is a bad note for the trumpet.
>
> The passage for Bass Trombone is dangerous - unless played by a very good performer.
>
> There is very little time for the Clarionets to change.
>
> In the Flute part this is not good. I would omit.

At one point Bishop's notes imply that Ouseley, feeling uneasy at some feature, must have prayed in his aid a precedent from Beethoven. This can be identified as the last chord of bar 6 and the first chord of bar 7 of the slow movement of the Piano Sonata Op.57, involving a technical point of some fascination. But the professor, true to his principles, will have none of it, writing:

> I cannot as to the 5ths agree to its being less objectionable because written by that great composer. However, in an Exercise submitted to me for a Degree I can only be guided by established rules:- rules which I cannot perceive any valid necessity for infringing.

And, for good measure, he goes on:

> Your progression, it may be observed, is not quite the same as Beethoven's - as to the 2nd chord he has added the 7th. Not that this, in my opinion, gives him any license [*sic*] for the consecutive 5ths.

APPENDIX D

Ouseley's private letter to Miller, 14 March 1857
(Domus MS 2) (see p.34)

Following the passage quoted, Ouseley continues:

It has pleased God in His goodness to endow me with a natural taste & facility in music & from my childhood I always wished to devote this gift to His service. This object I kept steadily in view throughout my Oxford career as an undergraduate & Bachelor [of Arts]. I determined, in prosecution of this object, to take a degree in the faculty of music, & then to be ordained a minister of the Church, believing that by these means I could best attain that object on which my dearest affections & hopes had so long rested, i.e. to do something to raise the music of the Sanctuary, & to devote to the service of God as much as possible of those gifts wh. He had given to me. When circumstances wh. you know of first put the idea of building St Michael's Church into my head, I saw as it were the hand of God in it, plainly directing me how to act. I saw in prospect the realization of all that I had hoped for, & I felt that the more God blessed the work in wh. I was engaged, the more it behoved me to strive to do my part towards the advancement of His Glory. I conceived that it was my special province to organize a model Choir-service, to try to devote the highest developments of that noble art & science of wh. I am so devoted a student to God's service, & therefore I was, and am, prepared to sacrifice, if need be, wealth, rank, comfort, everything in short, for the attainment of this object. I felt, & I think rightly, that many men might build churches, but few were able or willing to found model choirs, & my position as Professor of music at Oxford, & Precentor of Hereford rendered this conviction doubly urgent upon me. At the same time I felt that more ought to be done than to gather together a parcel of choristers, they ought to be educated, boarded, lodged, & it ought to be made useful in some way to some class or other out of wh. these boys shd. be taken. On reflection I thought that none had a higher claim on me than the sons or orphans of poor clergy, & accordingly I determined that we should board lodge & educate gratuitously eight boys, to be chosen according to their vocal fitness for the office of a chorister, but preference being always given to the sons or orphans of clergymen. Now to do this properly of course a College had to be built, a master found, & an annual sum of at least £400 provided. Others came forward & helped me. I am therefore sole trustee for part of this sum, & bound to support a certain number of boys to be choristers, & to whom I am bound to supply a liberal education. But funds lacked, this cd. not be made permanent without it were likewise selfsupporting. I have therefore determined to risk an experiment, & start a larger school than I at first contemplated, one to a great extent to be formed on the model of St Peter's Radley, tho' at the same time free from it's [*sic*] defects & extravagances. If God blesses this scheme as He has hitherto blessed my former endeavours, I have no fears for the result.

As to doctrine, I beg to state, for my own satisfaction as well as your's [*sic*], that I hate puritanism having seen too much of it in my youth, & on the other hand I have seen far too much both of Romanism, and of Romanizing Anglicanism, not to hate this extreme quite as cordially. I therefore hope and pray that in St Michael's College nothing but the pure & solid theology of the Church of England may be taught & that it may be strengthened to resist successfully the various baneful influences with wh. we are now so sorely beset on all sides.

I have now, my dear Sir, told my whole mind, my whole heart in this matter. I have written to you as a friend, hiding nothing, & I hope that if you can put yourself into my position for a moment, you will see that I could not very well act otherwise than I have acted without a very considerable sacrifice of principle & of conscience. Pray excuse the length of this letter, & pardon my egotism.

APPENDIX E
Non-resident Fellows under the original Statutes
(see p.35)

The Founder's own appointments are recorded in his hand in Domus MS 3. For the remainder up to the year 1916 reliance is placed on G.C.E.Ryley's compilation, Domus MS 7, the sources behind which are unknown.

APPOINTED BY THE FOUNDER

1856

James Wayland Joyce (1812-87)
MA Oxon. Sometime Student of Christ Church. Ouseley's lifelong most intimate friend. Rector of Burford, Salop (3rd portion), 1852-80.

Hubert McLaughlin
MA Dub. Rector of Burford, Salop (1st portion), 1838.

Henry Fyffe (*1816)
MA Oxon. Ouseley's fellow-curate at St Paul's, Knightsbridge and in charge of the establishment maintained by Ouseley at Lovehill House, Langley, Bucks. Subsequently Principal of St Helen's College, Southsea.

John Rich (1826-1913)
MA Oxon. Ouseley's friend from undergraduate days at Oxford. Subsequently Vicar of Chippenham and Rector of Kellaways. A trustee of Ouseley's residual estate.

John Jebb (1805-86)
DD Dub. Rector of Peterstow and Canon of Hereford Cathedral.

Edward John Ottley (1821-72)
Nephew of W.Y.Ottley, Keeper of Prints and Drawings in the British Museum. Presented MS conducting score of *Messiah*. A personal friend of Ouseley, apparently holding the rank of Captain.

Alfred Trevor Crispin (1822-92)
Of the legal department of the Treasury. Evidently a personal friend of Ouseley.

Edwin George Monk (1819-1900)
D Mus Oxon. Organist of St Peter's College, Radley, 1848, and York Minster, 1859-83. Regular co-examiner with Ouseley for Oxford degrees in music.

1857

Anthony Latouche Kirwan (1803-1868)
DD Dub. Dean of Limerick Cathedral, 1849. His two sons were original choristers of St Michael's.

William Sewell (1804-74)
DD Oxon. Fellow of Exeter College and White's Professor of Moral Philosophy. Parted with Tractarians on publication of Tract XC.

1858

Richard Whitmore Norman
BD, MA Oxon: DCL Toronto.. Assisted Henry Fyffe (above) at Lovehill House. Briefly Headmaster of St Michael's College, 1857. Subsequently Warden of St Peter's College, Radley and eventually Rector and Dean of the city and diocese of Quebec.

Thomas Thorp
MA, BD Cantab. Rector of Kemerton, Glos. (now Worcs.), where daily choral services were maintained.

1859

John Joseph Miller (1822-64)
MA Cantab. Nephew of T.E.Miller and John Miller (see p.24 above). Vicar of the family livings of Leysters (1855-64) and of Bockleton (1858-64).

Thomas Ayscough Smith (later T.A.Ayscough) (1831-1920)
MA Cantab. Vicar of Tenbury 1860-92, then Vicar of Cradley. A trustee of Ouseley's residual estate.

1860

William Magan Campion (†1896)
DD Cantab. Fellow of Queens' College, later President. His connection with the Founder and St Michael's is not apparent.

1861

Thomas Littleton Wheeler (†1910)
MA Oxon. Curate and assistant master of St Michael's, 1857-60. Honorary Canon of Worcester Cathedral, 1906, after work in the dioceses of Worcester and Hereford.

1862

John Capel Hanbury (*1833)
MA Oxon. Organist of St Michael's, 1856-7. Afterwards Chaplain of Wadham College, Oxford, and Hereford Chaplain at Wiesbaden.

(1862)

William James Earley Bennett (1804-86)

MA Oxon. Sometime Student of Christ Church. Eventually Vicar of Frome, Somerset. Ouseley served under him as an honorary curate in the parish of St Paul's, Knightsbridge, with the daughter church of St Barnabas, Pimlico.

Sir Henry Williams Baker, *Bt.* (1821-77)

MA Cantab. Vicar of Monkland, Herefordshire and the prime promoter of *Hymns Ancient and Modern.*

James Elwin Millard (1823-94)

MA Oxon. Chorister of Magdalen College, Oxford. Headmaster of Magdalen College School, 1846-64, and Fellow of Magdalen College. Afterwards Rector of Basingstoke. Brother of F.M.Millard below.

1864

Henry Aldrich Cotton (†1927)

MA Oxon. Curate and assistant master of St Michael's, 1860-62. Later Minor Canon of Westminster Abbey and Vicar of Stanford-in-the-vale, Berks.

Henry John Burfield (†1882)

MA Oxon. Vicar of St James's, Bradford and St Mark's, Leicester. A friend of Ouseley's from Oxford days. Buried at St Michael's.

1868

Robert Corbet Singleton (1810-81)

MA Dub. First Warden of St Peter's College, Radley, 1847-51 (see also Monk and Norman). There was apparently some feeling of kinship between St Peter's and St Michael's Colleges.

1872

Frederick Maule Millard (1835-1914)

MA Oxon. Headmaster of St Michael's College, 1862-9, afterwards Rector of Otham, Kent. Brother of J.E.Millard above.

1877

Marmaduke Charles Frederick Morris (1844-1935)

BCL, MA Oxon. Choral Scholar of New College, Oxford. Headmaster of St Michael's College, 1869-74. Subsequent career in the diocese of York. A trustee of Ouseley's residuary estate.

Vincent King Cooper (*c.*1850-1922)

MA Oxon. Headmaster of St Michael's College 1875-6. Subsequently Minor Canon, Precentor, and Honorary Canon of Durham Cathedral.

1881

John Samuel Sidebotham (1830-1901)

MA Oxon. Chaplain of New College, Oxford, 1853-66 and subsequently Vicar of Aymestrey, Herefordshire. First Honorary Librarian of St Michael's College, 1858-1901, and for many years editor of *Crockford's Clerical Directory.*

1883

Henry Chittenden Rogers (1835-1914)

MA Oxon. Headmaster of St Michael's College, 1876-79. Chaplain of Christ Church and Headmaster of Christ Church Cathedral School, 1879-84, and eventually Rector of Narborough.

1884

Edward Charles Corfe (†1937)

MA Oxon. An Old Boy of the College, 1863-68. Son of C. W. Corfe, organist of Christ Church Cathedral. Minor Canon of Rochester Cathedral and eventually Canon Residentiary of Truro Cathedral. Brother of C.J.Corfe (below).

1886

John Henry Mee (1852-1918)

MA, D Mus Oxon. Fellow of Merton College, Oxford; Precentor of Chichester Cathedral, 1889.

William Rayson (†1908)

MA Oxon. Curate of Kemerton (see Thomas Thorp above). Then Minor Canon of Worcester Cathedral; Vicar of Lindridge, Worcs., 1873-95.

1888

Charles John Corfe (1843-1921)

MA, Hon.DD Oxon. Came to St Michael's College from Lovehill House in 1856. Assistant master of St Michael's College, 1864-7, then Chaplain RN and eventually Bishop of Korea 1889-1905. Brother of E.C.Corfe (above.)

APPOINTED BY WARDEN HAMPTON

1893

Arthur Henry Saint Pattrick

MA Oxon. Assistant master of St Michael's College, 1877-82. Then Chaplain of Magdalen College and New College, Oxford and eventually Vicar of Washington, Essex.

1894

The Hon. James Wentworth Leigh (1838-1923)

DD Cantab. Dean of Hereford, 1894-1913.

William Claxton (†1933)

B Mus, MA Oxon. An Old Boy of the College, 1862-68. Organist. 1877-86. Eventually Vicar of Navestock, Essex. Resigned Fellowship on retirement, 1921.

Frederick William Joyce (1852-1934)

MA Oxon. An Old Boy of the College, 1864-65. Rector of Burford, Salop (1st Portion), then Vicar of Harrow and Prebendary of St Paul's Cathedral. Author of the Founder's biography (1896). Son of J.W.Joyce (above) and brother of J.B.Joyce (below). Buried at St Michael's.

Sir John Stainer (1840-1901)

MA, D Mus Oxon. Organist of the College, 1857-59. Afterwards Organist successively of Magdalen College, Oxford, and St Paul's Cathedral. Succeeded Ouseley as Professor of Music at Oxford. Knighted, 1888.

Arthur Hew (or Hugh) Dalrymple Prendergast (1833-1910)

MA Oxon. A solicitor who later devoted himself to music and was for many years Secretary of the (London) Bach Choir. A friend of St Michael's College from Ouseley's days.

(1894)

The Right Hon. John Francis Erskine Goodeve-Erskine, 27th Earl of Mar (1836-1930)

MA Cantab. As Mr J.F.E.Goodeve was an adult Commoner of the College for a term in 1866 prior to his ordination as deacon, immediately following which he succeeded to the earldom and proceeded no further in the ministry. His title, at first disputed, was recognised by the Earldom of Mar Restitution Act of 1885. He resigned his Fellowship somewhat before his death.

Charles Plummer (†1927)

MA Oxon, Hon DD Dunelm., Hon Litt D Dub., Hon D Litt Celt. National University of Ireland, FBA. An Old Boy of the College, 1863-65. Fellow and Chaplain (though not proceeding beyond the diaconate) of Corpus Christi College, Oxford. Ford's Lecturer in English History and author of some standard historical works.

James Barclay Joyce (†1934)

MA Oxon. An Old Boy of the College, 1864-65. Rector of Coreley, Salop. and Prebendary of Hereford Cathedral. Son of J.W.Joyce and brother of F.W.Joyce (above). His son, Geoffrey Michael Joyce, Rector of Burford (1st Portion) was elected a Fellow in 1943.

1902

Sir Walter Parratt, *KCVO* (1841-1924)

MA, D Mus Oxon. Organist successively of Magdalen College, Oxford and St George's Chapel, Windsor Castle. Master of the Queen's/King's Music. Professor of Music at Oxford, 1908-18. He had come to Ouseley's notice when organist at Witley Court, Worcs., 1861-68.

George Robertson Sinclair (1862-1917)

D Mus Lambeth. An Old Boy of the College, 1873-78. Organist of Truro Cathedral, then of Hereford Cathedral.

Alexander Frederick de Gex (1859-1931)

An Old Boy of the College, 1869-75, and son of Ouseley's fellow-curate at St Paul's, Knightsbridge. Ordained after first going in for banking, and became Rector of Meshaw and Creacombe, Devon, but retired after a breakdown in health in 1923.

1911

Frederick Bennett (1844-1933)

MA Oxon. Nephew of W.J.E.Bennett (above) whose biography he wrote, and known to Hampton from Pimlico days. Rector of Farleigh.

Geoffrey Charles Edward Ryley (1866-1947)

B Mus, MA Oxon. Assistant master at St Michael's College, 1895-96. Afterwards successively Minor Canon of Gloucester and Canterbury Cathedrals. ***WARDEN***, 1916. Eventually Honorary Canon of Rochester Cathedral.

APPOINTED BY WARDEN RYLEY

1916

John Hampton (1834-1921)

MA Cantab. Choirmaster, 1856-1916. ***WARDEN***, 1889-1916.

(1916)

Ernest Breffitt (*1862)

An Old Boy of the College, 1872-77. Iron merchant, of the firm of Scrivener, Breffitt and Co., Cardiff. His two brothers, afterwards clergymen, were also at St Michael's. He was the first Secretary of the St Michael's College Society. This appointment was of a markedly different character from any hitherto.

APPOINTED BY WARDEN SWANN

1918

Walter Howard Frere (1863-1938)

DD Cantab. Superior of the Community of the Resurrection, then Bishop of Truro. Eminently learned in liturgiology and liturgical music. He preached at Mr Buckmaster's installation as Warden in 1937.

(Sir) Percy Carter Buck (1871-1947)

MA, D Mus Oxon. Successively Organist of Wells and Bristol Cathedrals and Director of Music at Harrow School. Concurrently with work at Harrow, Professor of Music, University of Dublin, then in the University of London. Resigned Fellowship in 1933. Knighted in 1937.

1920

Edmund Horace Fellowes, *CH, MVO* (1870-1951)

B Mus, MA, Hon.D Mus Oxon, Hon.Mus D Dub. et Cantab. Honorary Librarian of the College, 1918-48. Precentor of Bristol Cathedral, then Minor Canon of St George's Chapel, Windsor Castle. The most noted English musical scholar of his day.

APPENDIX F

Service Lists for last complete week of October 1857, 1867, 1877, 1887

1857

Sun	Ouseley in A	God is our hope	Greene
M.	Rogers in D	The Lord descended	W. Hayes
	Rogers in D	Prepare ye the way	Wise
T.	Ouseley in E flat	I bow my knee	Beckwith
	Ouseley in E flat	O Lord, the maker	"Henry VIII"
W.	Aldrich in G	Rejoice in the Lord	Purcell
	Aldrich in G	Sing we merrily	Crotch
Th.	Travers in F	O God, forasmuch	Travers
	Travers in F	Save, Lord, and hear us	W. Hayes
F.	Bevin in D minor	How long wilt thou	Ouseley
	Bevin in D minor	Put me not to rebuke	Croft
S.	Ouseley in C [?]	O praise the Lord	Ouseley
	Ouseley in C [?]	O worship the Lord	W. Hayes

1867

Sun	Kelway in B minor	O praise the Lord with me	Ouseley
M.	Boyce in C	Enter not into judgment	Clarke
	Kelway in G minor	The Lord helpeth	Mozart
T.	Kempton in B flat	How dear are thy counsels	Crotch
	Kempton in B flat	Sing unto the Lord	Tye
W.	Gibbons in F	Try me, O God	Benedict
	Gibbons in F	By the waters of Babylon	Boyce
Th.	Nares in F	O be joyful	Greene
	Nares in F	The Lord is my shepherd	Ouseley
F.	Ouseley in B minor	Hide not thou thy face	Farrant
	Ouseley in B minor	O Lord my God	Bull
S.	King in C	Righteous art thou	P. Hayes
	King in C	Lift up your heads	Gibbons

1877

Sun.	Goss in E	The Wilderness	Goss
M.	Boyce in C	I was glad	Elvey
	Kelway in B minor	The glory of the Lord	Goss
T.	Smart in F	Above all praise	Mendelssohn
	Smart in F	How goodly are thy tents	Ouseley
W.	Ouseley in A	Try me, O God	Benedict
	Ouseley in A	The king shall rejoice	Hopkins
Th.	King in F	Love not the world	Ouseley
	King in F	Sing, O heavens	Sullivan
F.	Rogers in F	Rend your hearts	Ouseley
	Rogers in F	Thou judge of quick and dead	S.S. Wesley
S.	Nares in F	Come unto me	Stafford Smith
	Nares in F	The earth is the Lord's	Spohr

1887

Sun.	Colborne in B flat	Sing, O daughter of Sion	Ouseley
M.	Garrett in F	How dear are thy counsels	Crotch
	Garrett in F	The Lord hath done	Smart
T.	Boyce in A (verse)	Behold now, praise the Lord	Aldrich
	Kelway in A minor	If ye then be risen	Naylor
W.	Gates in F	Let thy merciful ears	Gaul
	Foster in F	Put me not to rebuke	Croft
Th.	Rogers in E minor	Let the wicked	Goss
	Rogers in E minor	O be joyful	W. Hayes
F.	Ouseley in A	The Lord preserveth	Armes
	Ouseley in A	Sing praises to the Lord	Croft
S.	Stewart in G	O Lord our governor	P. Hayes
	Stewart in G	It shall come to pass	Garrett

APPENDIX G
Repertory of Services & Anthems in 1865 and 1885
Column A - 1865; Column B - 1885

I. SERVICES
*-Morning only. †-Evening only

	A	B
ALDRICH (Henry) *1647-1710*		
in G	8	6
ARNOLD (Samuel) *1740-1802*		
†in A	10	8
in D	1	0
ATTWOOD (Thomas) *1765-1838*		
in F	2	5
BARROW (Thomas) *d.1789*		
in F	6	6
BATTEN (Adrian) *1591-1637*		
in D minor	6	4
BLOW (John) *1649-1708*		
in A	4	0
BOYCE (William) *1710-1779*		
*in A	10	8
*in A (Verse)	2	4
*in C	8	5
BOYCE (William) & HAYES (William)		
†in G	0	5
BRYAN (Albertus) *d. c1668*		
in G	9	4
CHILD (William) *1606-1697*		
in F	5	0
in G	8	4
CLAXTON (William) *d.1933; Prob.& Chor.1862-8; Org.1877-86*		
in G	0	1
in E flat	3	0
COLBORNE (Langdon) *1837-89; Org.1860-74*		
in B flat	0	4
in C	0	4
in D	7	4
COOKE (Robert) *1768-1814*		
†in C	2	0
CREIGHTON (Robert) *c1639-1734*		
in E flat	6	6
in F minor	0	3
CROFT (William) *1678-1727*		
*in A	9	4
*in B minor	0	4
in E flat	3	0
DEANE (Thomas) *early 18th-cent.*		
*in C	2	6
ELVEY (George Job) *1816-93*		
†in A	9	5
in F	6	4
FARRANT (John) *16-17th cent.*		
in D minor	3	0
FARRANT (Richard) *c1530-1580*		
in G minor	6	5
FOSTER (John) *b.1827*		
†in F	10	5
GARRETT (George Mursell) *1834-96*		
in D	0	7
in F	0	4
GATES (Bernard) *1685-1773*		
*in F	10	5
GIBBONS (Orlando) *1583-1625*		
in F	10	2
GOSS (John) *1800-80*		
†in E	5	6
GREENE (Maurice) *1695-1755*		
in C	1	0
HALL (Henry) *1655-1707* & HINE (William) *1687-1730*		
*in E flat	2	5
HAYES (William) *1707-77*		
†in E flat	2	5

HOPKINS (Edward John) *1818-1901*		
in A	0	2
*in C	0	6
in F	7	3
KELWAY (Thomas) *d.1749*		
†in A minor	2	4
†in B minor	1	5
†in G minor	4	5
KEMPTON (Thomas) *1694-1762*		
in B flat	9	8
KING (Charles) *1687-1748*		
in C	8	6
in D	3	0
in F	9	6
MENDELSSOHN (Felix) *1809-47*		
in A	0	1
NARES (James) *1715-83*		
in A	7	5
OUSELEY (Frederick Arthur Gore) *1825-89*		
in A	5	5
†in B flat	0	6
in B minor	9	5
in E flat	3	6
in E	4	1
PATRICK (Nathaniel) *d.1595*		
in G minor	11	4
PRENDERGAST (Arthur Hew Dalrymple) *1833-1910*		
†in F	0	6
ROGERS (Benjamin) *1614-98*		
†in A minor	1	6
in D	8	7
in E minor	7	5
in F	8	4
in G (attrib.Peter Rogers)	7	4
RUSSELL (William) *1777-1813*		
†in A	3	0
SMART (Henry) *1813-79*		
†in B flat	0	4
in F	0	5
STAINER (John) *1840-1901*		
†in E flat	0	5
STEWART (Robert Prescott) *1825-94*		
in G	0	4
TALLIS (Thomas) *c1505-1585*		
in D minor	7	5
TRAVERS (John) *c1703-1758*		
in F	8	5
TURLE (James) *1802-82*		
in D	0	4
WALMISLEY (Thomas Attwood) *1814-56*		
†in B flat	6	4
in D	0	4
†in D minor	0	4
WESLEY (Samuel Sebastian) *1810-76*		
in E	0	4
in F	0	5

II. ANTHEMS

ALCOCK (John) *1715-1806*		
Wherewithall shall a young man	2	2
ALDRICH (Henry) *1647-1710*		
Behold now, praise the Lord	3	1
God is our hope and strength	2	1
Not unto us	1	2
O give thanks	3	4
Out of the deep	2	0
We have heard with our ears	2	0
ALEXANDER (Alfred) *b.1842; Org. 1874-7*		
The Lord upholdeth	0	2
Why seek ye the living	0	1
ARMES (Philip) *1836-1908*		
Give ear, O ye heavens	4	3
ATTWOOD (Thomas) *1765-1838*		
Come, Holy Ghost	3	4
Let the words of my mouth	2	1
Teach me, O Lord	3	0
They that go down to the sea	3	1

(Attwood, *cont.*)		
Turn thee again	2	1
Turn thy face	2	2
Withdraw not thou	0	1
BACH (J. S., *as attrib. by Ouseley*)		
Blessing and glory	4	0
I wrestle and pray	0	1
To Father, Son, and Holy Ghost	1	0
BARNBY (Joseph) *1838-96*		
Have mercy upon me	0	3
Let the words of my mouth	1	0
Make me a clean heart	0	1
It is high time	2	2
Sing and rejoice	0	1
The grace of God	0	1
BATTEN (Adrian) *1591-1637*		
Deliver us, O Lord	3	2
Hear my prayer, O God	1	3
O praise the Lord	0	2
BATTISHILL (Jonathan) *1738-1801*		
Call to remembrance	3	0
Deliver us, O Lord	2	1
O Lord, look down from heaven	3	2
BAUMER (Henry) *1835-88*		
Lord, how are they increased	1	0
BECKWITH (John Christmas) *1750-1809*		
I bow my knee	1	1
BENEDICT (Julius) *1804-85*		
Try me, O God	1	2
BENNETT (William Sterndale) *1816-75*		
Grant, we beseech thee	2	0
Great is our Lord	0	2
O that I knew	1	1
BLOW (John) *1649-1708*		
I was in the spirit	2	0
My God, my God	2	0
O God, wherefore art thou absent	3	0
Save me, O God	1	0
The Lord hear thee	4	5
BOYCE (William) *1710-79*		
All kings shall fall down	5	4
Blessing and glory	2	1
By the waters of Babylon	3	2
Lord, thou hast been our refuge	0	2
O give thanks	2	2
O where shall wisdom be found	2	1
Save me, O God	5	0
Teach me, O Lord	0	2
Turn thee unto me	4	1
Wherewithal shall a young man	2	2
BRIDGE (John Frederick) *1844-1924*		
Seek ye the Lord	0	3
The Lord hath chosen	0	2
BYRD (William) *c1543-1623*		
Bow thine ear	1	2
I will not leave you comfortless	2	0
CHAMPNEYS (Francis Henry) *b.1848*		
O praise the Lord	0	2
CHAWNER (C.F.Fox) *1840-67; Commoner (adult) 1863-7*		
Devout men carried Stephen	0	1
Draw nigh unto God	3	1
They that be wise	1	0
CHILD (William) *1606-97*		
O Lord, grant the king	1	0
Praise the Lord, O my soul	2	2
CLARKE (Jeremiah) *c1659-1707*		
O Lord God of my salvation	3	0
CLARKE [-WHITFELD] (John) *1770-1836*		
Enter not into judgment	0	3
CLARKE (?)		
The sorrows of death	1	2
CLAXTON (William) *d.1833; Prob. & Chor. 1862-8; Org. 1877-86*		
Blessed be the people	0	3
O Lord, we beseech thee	0	3
COLBORNE (Langdon) *1837-89; Org. 1860-74)*		
If thou shalt confess	0	3
Out of the deep	3	1
Ponder my words	2	3

CORFE (Charles William) *1814-83*		
Thou visitest the earth	2	0
COSTA (Michael) *1810-84*		
Lord, I have loved the habitation	0	3
COX (Hugh) *?19th century*		
Almighty God	2	0
CREIGHTON (Robert) *c1639-1734*		
I will arise	4	2
Praise the Lord, O my soul	2	2
CROFT (William) *1678-1727*		
Cry aloud and shout	2	2
God is gone up	3	4
O Israel, trust in the Lord	2	1
O Lord God of my salvation	2	0
O Lord, rebuke me not	0	1
O Lord, thou hast searched me out	1	1
O praise the Lord	3	0
Put me not to rebuke	2	2
Sing praises to the Lord	3	1
We will rejoice	4	4
CROTCH (William) *1775-1847*		
Be merciful	1	0
Comfort, O Lord, the soul	4	3
Holy, holy, holy	2	1
How dear are thy counsels	1	2
Sing we merrily	2	2
DUPUIS (Thomas Sanders) *1730-96*		
Not unto us	0	1
DYKES (John Bacchus) *1823-76*		
O God, forasmuch	2	3
These are they	1	1
ELVEY (George Job) *1816-93*		
Arise, shine	0	1
Be gracious	0	1
Christ being raised	1	1
In that day (1st part)	3	1
(2nd part)	1	0
I was glad	0	2
O do well	0	3
O give thanks	0	3
O praise the Lord of heaven	2	3
Rejoice in the Lord	0	2
Unto thee have I cried	2	2
Wherewithall shall a young man	2	2
EVANS (?William, *d.1740*)		
In thee, O Lord	1	0
FARRANT (Richard) *d.1580/1*		
Call to remembrance	2	3
Hide not thou thy face	3	3
Lord, for thy tender mercy's sake *(attrib.)*	2	1
FOX (William) *d.1579*		
Teach me thy way	1	1
GARRETT (George Mursell) *1834-96*		
It shall come to pass	0	1
Praise the Lord	0	2
GAUL (Alfred Robert) *1837-1913*		
Let thy merciful ears	0	1
This is the day	0	1
GAUNTLETT (Henry John) *1806-76*		
This is the day	1	0
Thou wilt keep him	1	0
GIBBONS (Orlando) *1583-1625*		
Almighty and everlasting God	3	3
God is gone up	1	0
Hosanna to the Son of David	2	0
Lift up your heads	1	1
O thou, the central orb (O all true faithful hearts)	0	2
This is the record of John	0	1
Why art thou so heavy	3	1
GOLDWIN (John) *1670-1719*		
I have set God	1	1
GOSS (John) *1800-80*		
Almighty and merciful Lord	4	0
Behold, I bring you glad tidings	0	1
Blessed is the man	3	1
Christ our Passover	0	1

(Goss, *cont.*)		
Come, and let us return	0	2
Fear not, O land	0	1
God so loved the world	2	2
If we believe that Jesus died	2	0
In Christ dwelleth	2	1
I will magnify	1	1
Let the wicked	2	1
O give thanks	0	2
O Lord God, thou strength	4	2
O praise the Lord of heaven	0	3
O Saviour of the world	0	1
O taste and see	4	2
Praise the Lord, O my soul	4	1
Stand up and bless the Lord	1	2
The glory of the Lord	0	2
These are they	0	1
The Wilderness	0	2
GREENE (Maurice) *1695-1755*		
Acquaint thyself with God	0	2
Cry aloud and shout	4	1
God is our hope and strength	2	0
How long wilt thou forget me	2	0
I have longed for thy saving health	2	0
I will lay me down	2	2
I will sing of thy power	2	3
Let God arise	3	1
Let my complaint	2	3
O be joyful	4	2
O clap your hands	2	1
O Lord, give ear	2	3
O Lord God of hosts	3	2
O sing unto the Lord	2	0
Praise the Lord, ye servants	2	1
Thou, O God, art praised in Zion	1	1
Thou visitest the earth	0	1
Try me, O God	1	0
HANDEL (G. F.) *1685-1759*		
And he shall purify	0	1
For unto us	1	1
Let all the angels of God	0	1
Lift up your heads	0	2
Since by man came death	0	1
The Lord gave the word	1	1
HASLER (?Hans Leo, *1564-1612*)		
If the Lord himself	3	2
HATTON (John Liptrott) *1809-86*		
I will praise thee	2	1
HAYDN (Franz Josef) *1732-1809*		
The heavens are telling	0	2
HAYES (Philip) *1738-97*		
I will magnify thee	2	2
O Lord our governor	1	1
Righteous art thou	0	1
The Lord descended	2	0
HAYES (William) *1707-77*		
Great is the Lord	4	6
Lord, thou hast been our refuge	4	2
O be joyful	2	1
O Lord God of hosts	1	0
O Lord our governor	1	0
O worship the Lord	4	2
Praise the Lord, O Jerusalem	3	1
Save, Lord, and hear us	2	2
HILES (? Henry *b.1826*)		
I will lay me down in peace	0	1
HOPKINS (Edward John) *1818-1901*		
In my distress	2	1
I will wash	0	1
Let us now go	1	1
Try me, O God	2	1
Why seek ye the living	0	1
HUMFREY (Pelham) *1647-74*		
Rejoice in the Lord, O ye righteous	1	2
KENT (James) *1700-76*		
Blessed be thou	2	2

LESLIE (Henry David) *1822-96*		
Blow ye the trumpet	2	2
O have mercy	1	0
LONGHURST (William Henry) *1819-1904*		
I cried unto the Lord	1	0
MACFARREN (George Alexander) *1813-87*		
The Lord is my shepherd	3	1
McLAUGHLIN (?)		
God is our hope	1	0
MANN (Richard) *1837-69; Lay Clerk 1857-64*		
Grant, we beseech thee	0	3
MENDELSSOHN (Felix) *1809-47*		
Above all praise	0	1
Cast thy burden	3	1
Hark, the herald angels sing	1	0
Hear my prayer	0	1
He that shall endure to the end	3	3
How lovely are the messengers	0	1
I waited for the Lord	0	4
Judge me, O God	0	4
Let our hearts be joyful	0	1
My God, my God	2	0
Now we are ambassadors	0	2
See what love hath the father	0	1
Sleepers, wake	3	1
MONK (Edwin George) *1819-1900*		
Great and marvellous	1	1
MONK (William Henry) *1823-89*		
If ye love me	0	1
MOZART (Wolfgang Amadeus) *1756-91*		
The Lord helpeth them (*arr. S.S.Wesley*)	4	1
MUNDY (William) *late 16th-cent.*		
O Lord, the maker (*attrib. Henry VIII*)	2	2
NARES (James) *1715-83*		
Blessed is he	2	1
The souls of the righteous	2	4
Try me, O God	2	2
NAYLOR (John) *1838-97*		
If ye then be risen	0	1
OAKELEY (Herbert Stanley) *1830-1903*		
O God, who hast prepared	1	0
Whatsoever is born of God	1	0
OUSELEY (Frederick Arthur Gore) *1825-1889*		
All the kings of the earth	0	2
And there was a pure river	1	1
Ascribe unto the Lord	0	1
Ascribe ye greatness	0	2
Awake, thou that sleepest	1	0
Blessed be thou	2	0
Christ is risen from the dead	1	1
From the rising of the sun	4	3
Happy is the man	0	1
Haste thee, O God	2	2
Hear, O Lord	0	2
How goodly are thy tents	1	5
I know that the Lord is great	2	2
In God's word	0	1
In Jewry is God known	0	1
Is it nothing to you	1	1
Like as the hart	0	3
Lord, I call upon thee	0	1
Love not the world	0	2
O God, wherefore art thou absent	0	1
O how plentiful	3	1
O love the Lord	4	2
O praise the Lord with me	2	3
O Saviour of the world	2	1
Save me, O God	2	2
Sing, O daughter of Zion	2	1
Sing unto the Lord	0	1
The Lord is king	2	0
The Lord is my shepherd	2	1
They that wait upon the Lord	2	1
Thou art my portion	0	5
Thy mercy, O Lord	2	0
Why standest thou so far off	3	1
PURCELL (Henry) *1659-95*		
O God, thou art my God	4	1

(Purcell, *cont.*)		
O sing unto the Lord	2	0
Remember not, Lord	1	0
Thou knowest, Lord	3	1
Thy word is a lantern	2	2
REDFORD (John) *early 16th cent.*		
Rejoice in the Lord	1	0
RICHARDSON (Vaughan) *1670-1729*		
O how amiable	2	0
ROGERS (Benjamin) *1614-98*		
Behold, how good and joyful	0	1
Behold now, praise the Lord	2	2
Lord, who shall dwell	2	2
O pray for the peace of Jerusalem	3	1
Praise the Lord, O my soul	0	1
Save me, O God	0	3
Teach me, O Lord	3	3
SCOTT (John) *1776-1815*		
Praise the Lord, O Jerusalem	3	3
SMART (Henry) *1813-79*		
O God, the king of glory	1	0
Sing unto the Lord	0	1
The Lord hath done great things	0	2
SMITH (John Stafford) *1750-1836*		
Come unto me	1	2
SMITH (George Townsend) *1813-77*		
If ye then be risen	0	1
SPARK (William) *1825-97*		
All we, like sheep	2	2
O God, have mercy	1	0
SPOHR (Louis) *1784-1859*		
As pants the hart	0	1
Behold, he shall come	0	1
Behold, I come	0	1
Holy, holy, holy	0	1
O may thy will be done	0	1
The earth is the Lord's	0	2
STAINER (John) *1840-1901*		
Deliver me, O Lord	1	1
Rejoice ye with Jerusalem	1	0
Sing a song of praise	0	3
The morning stars	1	1
The righteous live	4	2
What are these	0	1
STEGGALL (Charles) *1826-1905*		
God came from Teman	2	1
Hear ye, and give ear	4	2
O clap your hands	0	1
Remember now thy creator	0	2
STEWART (Robert Prescott) *1825-94*		
If ye love me	3	1
In the Lord put I my trust	4	1
Thou, O God, art praised in Sion	1	2
STROUD (Charles) *1706-26*		
Hear my prayer	2	3
SULLIVAN (Arthur Seymour) *1842-1900*		
I will mention	0	3
O love the Lord	3	3
O taste and see	0	1
Sing, O heavens	0	3
TALLIS (Thomas) *c1505-85*		
All people that on earth do dwell (*attrib.*)	5	2
Come, Holy Ghost (*attrib.*)	2	4
Hear the voice and prayer	2	1
If ye love me	3	2
TRAVERS (John) *c1703-56*		
Ascribe unto the Lord	0	1
If the Lord himself	2	1
TRIMNELL (Thomas Tallis) *1827-97*		
The Lord is king	0	1
TUCKER (William) *c1630-78*		
O give thanks	4	2
TUCKERMAN (Samuel Parkman) *1819-90*		
Turn thy face	1	0
TYE (Christopher) *c1497-c1572*		
Let thy loving mercy	3	2
O Lord, thy word (*adapt.*P. Hayes)	2	2
The proud have digged pits	3	1

VICTORIA (Tomás Luis de) *c1548-1611*		
Out of the deep	0	1
WALMISLEY (Thomas Attwood) *1814-56*		
Awake, awake	1	0
Father of heaven	2	0
If the Lord himself	1	0
Not unto us	2	0
O God, the king of glory	3	0
The Lord shall comfort Zion	2	0
WARD (C.R.) *?19th-cent.*		
Out of the deep	0	1
WEELKES (Thomas) *c1575-1623*		
All people, clap your hands	1	0
WELDON (John) *1676-1736*		
Hear my crying	3	0
In thee, O Lord	2	1
O praise God in his holiness	2	3
O praise the Lord	2	3
WESLEY (Samuel Sebastian) *1810-76*		
Blessed are they (from 'O give thanks')	2	2
Blessed be the God and Father	5	2
Cast me not away	1	0
For this mortal (from 'O Lord, thou art my God')	2	1
I am thine	0	1
Lead me, Lord	0	1
O Lord my God	4	0
The Lord hath been mindful (from 'Ascribe unto the Lord')	4	4
The Lord redeemed (from 'The face of the Lord')	2	2
The Wilderness	2	0
Thou judge of quick and dead (from 'Let us lift up our heart')	2	2
Thou wilt keep him	3	0
Wash me throughly	2	0
WISE (Michael) *c1648-87*		
Awake, put on thy strength	3	4
Awake up, my glory	2	1
Prepare ye the way	2	2
The ways of Zion	2	0
WORGAN (John) *1724-90*		
Easter Hymn	1	0

APPENDIX H
Two Ouseley mysteries

1. In the School Register of Hurstpierpoint College printed in 1914 there occurs, with vague reference apparently to *c*1853, the entry:

> Sir F. Gore Ouseley, Bt. Precentor. Afterwards Regius [sic] Professor of Music at Oxford Univ.

So far as can be made out, this seems to rest only on some reminiscences contributed to *The Hurst-Johnian* for 1911 by E. S. Churton, who was at Hurstpierpoint in 1853 and who said:

> Our first precentor was Frederick Gore Ouseley, precentor *pro tem.* as he styled himself, a most lovable and popular man. He was an enthusiast and taught me more genuine Church music than I ever learnt afterwards.

It is greatly to be doubted whether any reliance can be placed on this. No such episode in Ouseley's life is so much as hinted at in Joyce's biography, and he was almost certainly too occupied with schemes of his own in 1853 to have joined the staff, even temporarily and in an unpaid capacity, of Hurstpierpoint. I am kindly informed by Mr Christopher Dean, who raised this matter with me, that Ouseley does not appear in the ledger of salaried members of staff during the years 1852-54. Dare one speculate that, being interested in such a Church of England scholastic foundation, Ouseley briefly visited Hurstpierpoint and while there not unnaturally gave a little help with the choir; and that any such slight episode became magnified in Churton's mind long year after? Perhaps as Sir Frederick began he said something like 'Now think of me as your precentor *pro tem.*' He may perhaps have been visiting his friend John Rich, whose address, at anyrate by 1861, was New Timber, Hurstpierpoint. On the other hand, that Churton surprisingly fails to use Ouseley's title makes one wonder whether there has been some confusion of names.

What is interesting, Hurstpierpoint being a College of the Woodard Corporation, is that one of its pupils should have been so impressed by Ouseley. Nathaniel Woodard's biographer, Oates, records that Woodard himself deplored what Ouseley stood for in church music.

2. In the Church of St Margaret of Scotland, Aberlour, Banffshire (consecrated in 1877) there is a pair a lancet stained glass windows close to the organ. One of them depicts St Cecilia, the other St Gregory, and beneath both runs the inscription:

> A.M.D.G. et in carissimam memoriam Rev. Can. Sir F.A.G.Ouseley Bart. Mus.Doc.Oxon. 1890

Why Sir Frederick Ouseley should be thus commemorated on the banks of the River Spey is a mystery. Mr Donald Finlay, who has been kind enough to draw my attention to these windows, mentions that the Revd F.E.Scott, who had been organist and choirmaster of St Chad's College, Denstone, was assistant curate at Aberlour 1889-90. Mr Finlay therefore suggests that Scott's musical interests might explain matters. In 1889 he gave a window to St Margaret's in memory of his parents, and so Mr Finlay wonders whether perhaps it was he who put in the Ouseley windows also. If this be so it seems an extraordinary and tenuous link. Scott returned to Denstone after leaving Aberlour. There is no known connection between him and Ouseley or St Michael's College or between St Margaret's Church and Ouseley. Whoever was responsible for the windows felt close enough to Sir Frederick to use the word *carissimam*.

APPENDIX J
Wardens and Organists, 1856-1985

I. WARDENS (for further biographical details, see Chapters 2-4,6,7.)

1856-89 *Sir* Frederick (Arthur Gore) Ouseley, *Bt.*, MA, D Mus, Hon.LL D.

1889-1916 John Hampton, MA.

1916 Geoffrey Charles Edward Ryley, B Mus, MA.

1917-36 Ernest Henry Swann, MA.

1936-46 Cuthbert Harold Septimus Buckmaster.
Afterward Chaplain, RN.

[1940-45. Albert Victor Billen, DD, Acting Warden]

1947-56 Noel Henry Kemp-Welch, MA.
Probationer and Chorister of the College, 1919-24. Afterwards Senior Chaplain, St Peter's School, York.

1957-65 Desmond William Adair Stride, MA.
Afterwards Chaplain, Heathfield School, Ascot.

1965-77 Denis James Paxman, MA.
Afterwards successively Chaplain, Howell's School, Denbigh, Vicar of Lakenham, Suffolk, Rector of St Andrew's, Tain, Ross-shire.

1977-85 Andrew Farrar Walters, ACP.
Afterwards Headmaster, Homefield School, Sutton.

II. ORGANISTS (also, from early 1934, Choirmasters)

1856-57 John Capel Hanbury
See Appendix E.

1857-59 *(Sir)* John Stainer
See Appendix E.

1860-74 Langdon Colborne
1835-89. Pupil of George Cooper. Mus B Cantab. Afterwards o. of Beverley Minster, Wigan Parish Church, Dorking Parish Church, and finally of Hereford Cathedral. D Mus Lambeth.

1874-77 Alfred Alexander
b.1842. Chorister in Rochester Cathedral and pupil of John Hopkins. Minor appointments before St Michael's. Then o. of Wigan Parish Church, American Church in Nice, and St Andrew's, Southport.

1877-86 William Claxton
See Appendix E.

1886-89 Walter James Lancaster
b.1860. Pupil of E.J.Hopkins. Earlier o. of Dover Parish Church and All Saints', Kingston on Thames. Afterwards o. of Bolton Parish Church, Lancs., FRCO, and Mus B Manchester.

1889-93 Allan Paterson
b.1865. Formerly assistant o. of Hereford Cathedral under Colborne. Afterwards o. of Malvern Priory, Govan Parish Church, St Paul's, Cannes, and St Paul's, Greenock. FRCO and Mus B Dublin.

1894 Charles Harry Moody *(CBE)*
1874-1965. Articled pupil at Bangor Cathedral. Easter Term only at St Michael's. Afterwards o. of Wigan Parish Church, Holy Trinity, Coventry, and then of Ripon Cathedral. D Mus Lambeth.

1894-96 James Lyon
b.1872. Formerly Sub-o. of Bangor Cathedral. Afterwards music master of Warwick School, then o. of Wallasey Parish Church, Lancs. before settling in Birmingham. After leaving St Michael's, took Oxford degrees of B Mus and D Mus.

1896-1907 Edgar C. Broadhurst
1876-1967. Formerly chorister and assistant o. of Hereford Cathedral under Sinclair. Afterwards o. of Harrow Parish Church (Vicar, F.W.Joyce: see Appendix E) and taught at Harrow School. Late in life for his second wife he married a daughter of John Hampton. Fellow of the College, 1953.

1908-1909 Maurice Gordon Burgess
1884-1964. BA, B Mus Oxon, FRCO. Undergraduate o. of Wadham College, Oxford. Silver Medal, Worshipful Company of Musicians. Afterwards o. of Dulwich College.

1910 Percy C. Davis
Emigrated to the USA.

1911-12 Norman Charles Wood
1882-1944. MA, Mus B Cantab, FRCO. Formerly o. of Ludlow Parish Church. Afterwards o. of Holy Trinity, Southport, Minor Canon of Winchester Cathedral and Headmaster of the Cathedral Choir School, and eventually Vicar of St John the Evangelist, Notting Hill, London.

1913-18 Arthur John Baynon
1889-1954. B Mus, FRCO. Formerly Music Master of Truro College. Afterwards Director of Music at Caterham School. During absence on war service his place was temporarily supplied by Messrs Carlton Borrow (1917) and Vivian Stuart (1918).

1919 (Sir) Ernest Bullock *(CVO)*
1890-1979. D Mus Dunelm, FRCO. Formerly assistant o. of Manchester Cathedral, afterwards o. of Exeter Cathedral and Westminster Abbey. Director of the Royal College of Music. Fellow of SMC, 1936.

1920-25 Heathcote Dicken Statham *(CBE)*
1889-1973. Mus D Cantab, FRCO. Old Boy of the College, 1899-1904. Formerly o. of Calcutta Cathedral. Afterwards o. of Southampton Parish Church and Norwich Cathedral. Fellow of the College, 1949.

1925-31 Stanley Thorne
d.c1970. FRCO. Pupil of Ernest Bullock. Afterwards Music Master of St George's College, Buenos Aires, Leighton Park School, Reading, and the Friends' School, Saffron Walden. Eventually County Music Organiser for Northamptonshire.

1931-35 Laurence Crossthwaite
1906-86. B Mus, MA Oxon, FRCO. Formerly Director of Music, Bishop Cotton School, Simla, afterwards at Stamford School and Bromsgrove School.

1935-52 Maxwell Graham Menzies
B Mus, MA Oxon, FRCO. Probationer and Chorister of the College, 1923-26. Organ Exhibitioner of St John's College, Oxford. Afterwards o. of Maidstone Parish Church, Portsmouth Cathedral, and eventually on staff of Birmingham School of Music. During his absence on war service Sir Sydney Nicholson and Mr C.E.S.Littlejohn acted as organists.

1952-59 Kenneth Bernard Beard
Mus B Manchester, MA Cantab, FRCO. Organ Scholar of Emmanuel College, Cambridge. Afterwards o. and Rector Chori of Southwell Cathedral.

1959-72 Lucian Nethsingha
MA Cantab, FRCO. Afterwards o. of Exeter Cathedral

(Joint post of Choirmaster and Organist now designated Master of the Music)

1973-1985 Roger Lewin Judd
MA Cantab, FRCO. Formerly chorister of Winchester Cathedral, Organ Scholar of Pembroke College, Cambridge, and assistant o. of Ely Cathedral. Afterwards Sub-o. of St George's Chapel, Windsor Castle.

APPENDIX K
Iconography at St Michael's College
(excluding photography)

The following (dimensions in inches) were in the Library or Dining Hall:

1. **Aldrich** (Henry) *1647-1710.* Half length. Right shoulder to onlooker, black clothes with bands, no wig. Clearly related to Kneller's portrait at Christ Church, Oxford, though facing the other way and so perhaps taken from the engraving in reverse by Smith. In oils on canvas, 29" x 24½." Painter unknown.

2. (*said to be*) **Blow** (John) *1649-1708.* Head and shoulders facing directly to front. Full heavy countenance, lace cravat, and wig. Obviously of some late 17th-century figure, but identification very doubtful. In oils on canvas, 18" x 14½." Ascription to Sir Peter Lely unauthenticated. Reproduced in *John Blow. Deux Sonates...Publiées par W.Gillies Whittaker* (Paris, 1933).

3. **Corfe** (*Bishop* Charles John) *1843-1921.* Head and shoulders facing to onlooker's right. Bearded, with clerical collar. Inscribed in top left-hand corner beneath a heraldic shield: 'Right Reverend Charles J. Corfe, D.D./ Missionary Bishop in Corea and Manchuria'. In oils on canvas, 25" x 21." Artist unknown.

4. **Hampton** (John) *1834-1921.* Three-quarter length. Seated facing front, elbows on arms of chair. In later life, white hair and beard, spectacled. Black clothes and flowing white tie. Cross hanging from watch chain. Seated in chair with brass knobs on arms. In oils on canvas, 49" x 39." Artist unknown. Though closely similar in pose, the photograph facing p.54 of A&C is not a reproduction of this.

5. **Handel** (George Frideric) *1685-1759.* Half length. Seated facing front, holding copy of music in L.H. Wig, lace cuffs, embroidered coat. Obviously an inferior copy of portrait by Thomas Hudson now in Hamburg. In oils on canvas, 34½ x 27. Painter unknown. A somewhat similar copy is in the Bodleian Library.

6. **Hayes** (Philip) *1738-97.* Small full length. Seated with copy of his oratorio *Prophecy* before him, wearing wig. knee breeches, buckled shoes and the dress of an Oxford Doctor of Music. In oils on canvas, 17 x 12½. Artist unknown.

7. **Ouseley** (*Sir* Frederick Arthur Gore, *2nd Baronet*) 1825-89. Small head and shoulders, facing over right shoulder. Fair wavy hair, as a child of about ten years or less. Small, lightly tinted drawing on paper, 6½ x 5½ within the mount. By H.B.Ziegler, stated to be c1835. *Now deposited with RSCM at Addington Palace, Croydon.*

8. **The same**. Full length. Seated at pianoforte, hands on keyboard, left wrist slightly raised. Facing onlooker over right shoulder. Wavy hair, white lace collar, white ankle-length drawers showing below plum-coloured smock-like dress. In oils on canvas, 58 x 44. By R.A.Lucas. Stated to have been exhibited at the Royal Academy. Reproduced in Joyce (frontispiece), A&C (facing p.6), and in E. H. Fellowes, *The Catalogue of Manuscripts in the Library of St Michael's College Tenbury* (Paris, 1934). *Now deposited with RCO, Kensington Gore, London SW7.*

9. **The same.** Full length. Standing, left shoulder to onlooker, left hand lightly resting on table. Scroll with seal on his right. Romantically ample robe (and hood) of an Oxford Doctor of Music, wearing bands. Round the frame, legends of Ouseley's positions as Founder of St Michael's College, Incumbent of St Michael's, Professor of Music at Oxford, and Precentor of Hereford Cathedral. In oils on canvas, 1857, 94 x 58. By W.H.Florio Hutchinson, drawing master at St Peter's College, Radley. Presented by the Warden and Fellows of St Peter's College. See Havergal, p.69.

10. **The same.** Bust, in later life. In clay. By H.J.Bailey of Rowden Abbey, Bromyard. See Joyce, p.178.

11. **Ouseley** (*Sir* Gore, *1st Baronet*) *1770-1844.* Head and shoulders. Right shoulder slightly towards onlooker, fresh complexion, clean shaven, age perhaps 40. In oils on canvas, 29½ x 24½. *Now deposited with the Bodleian Library, Oxford.*

REFERENCES

Except where otherwise noted, all MSS and books are deposited in the care of Hereford Cathedral Library.

A MANUSCRIPT

Domus MS 1 — Year lists, in an unidentified hand, of members of Ouseley's intended foundation from March 1851 (at Lovehill House, Langley, Bucks) to 1858 (overlapping the first few years at Tenbury). The earlier years were probably written up retrospectively. It should be noted that the details given for 1856-7-8 do not tally exactly with Ouseley's own careful lists in Domus MS 3.

Domus MS 2 — Letters relating to negotiations leading up to the establishment of St Michael's Church and College. Provenance uncertain. They had been brought and placed on the table in the College library in 1964, but by whom was not discovered. The guess is now hazarded that, along with Domus MS 1, they may have been among the papers of the late Cyril Joyce, brother of F.W.Joyce (Ouseley's biographer) and himself for long a trustee of St Michael's College.

3 Sept. [18]52. The Revd J. W. Joyce presumably to the Revd John Miller of Bockleton.
3 Sept, 1852. Sir Frederick Ouseley presumably to John Miller.
7 Sept. 1852. John Miller to Sir Frederick Ouseley (with copy).
11 Sept. 1852. The same to the same.
16 Sept. 1852. Sir Frederick Ouseley to John Miller.
15 Nov. 1852. The same to the same.
18 Jan. 1853. J. W. Joyce to John Miller.
14 May 1853. J. W. Joyce presumably to either T. E. or John Miller.
17 May 1853. File copy, with tracing of map, from William Norris, solicitor, to John Miller.
20 May 1853. File copy from William Norris to John Miller.
17 Jan. 1855. Sir Frederick Ouseley to T. E. Miller.
10 Mar. 1857. Private letter from John Miller to Sir Frederick Ouseley, with printed copy of letters publicly exchanged between them, 13 and 14 March 1857.
14 Mar. 1857. Private letter from Sir Frederick Ouseley to John Miller.

Domus MS 3 — Terminal Register of the Foundation, laid out like a college entry in a University Calendar, 1856-1892 with some addenda. In Sir Frederick Ouseley's hand until his death.

Domus MS 4 — Register of pupils admitted to St Michael's College.
(a) 1856-1951
(b) 1951-1985

Domus MS 5 — Register of music sung and attendances at Services.

(a) Feb. 1857-July 1862
(b) Aug. 1862-July 1870
(c) Sept. 1870-Dec. 1895
(d) Feb. 1896-Dec. 1905
(e) Jan. 1906 - July 1915
(f) Sept. 1915 - Dec. 1922
(g) Jan. 1923 - July 1930
(h) Sept. 1930 - March 1940
(j) May 1940 - Dec. 1950
(k) Jan. 1951 - Dec. 1971
(l) Jan. 1972 - July 1985

Domus MS 6 — List of preachers and music at Commemoration 1856-1957 with some additions, mainly compiled by John Skelton Bumpus.

Domus MS 7 — Biographical notices of the Fellows of St Michael's College, 1856-1943, initiated by the Revd G. C. E. Ryley.

Domus MS 8 — Bound volume of letters from Sir Frederick Ouseley to Canon Frederick Alderson and his son Montague Frederick Alderson.

Hampton MS — Two reminiscent memoranda compiled in old age by the Revd John Hampton together with a copy letter from him to A. S. Miles dated 19 Sept. [19]17, now in the possession of his grandson. A typed transcript is deposited as Domus MS 9 in Hereford Cathedral Library.

N&M MS 1 — Receipt from building contractor, now among papers held by Messrs Norris and Miles, Solicitors, Market Square, Tenbury Wells, Worcs.

N&M MS 2 — Draft of proposed appeal, 1868, in the hand of Sir Frederick Ouseley, now held by Messrs Norris and Miles.

N&M MS 3 — Rough cash book kept by A.S. Miles, Aug. 1878-Oct. 1884, held by Messrs Norris and Miles.

Ouseley MS 1 — Bound quarto album in the hand of Sir Gore Ouseley and illustrated heraldically giving some account of his own genealogy (traced through his great-great-grandmother, Magdalen Wake, to a cousin of William the Conqueror) and also (pp.13-19) some autobiographical detail.

Ouseley MS 2 — Bound folio album stamped *PARENTALIA* compiled by Sir Gore Ouseley and illustrated heraldically, displaying his descent from Charlemagne.

Ouseley MS 3 — A bound folio volume, thumb indexed, complied by Sir Gore Ouseley and illustrated heraldically, setting out his descent from some hundred or more illustrious families.

Ouseley MS 4 — A volume similar to Ouseley MS 2, but extra-illustrated.

Ouseley MS 5 — A small quarto volume in the hand of Sir Bulstrode Whitelocke (1605-75). The present calf binding has blind stamped patterns of early Victorian gothic style. *Now deposited in the Bodleian Library, Oxford.*

Ouseley MS 6 — A large quarto bound album, being an 18th-century transcript made from the holograph of Sir James Whitelocke (†1632) of his *Liber Familicus, 1609-31.* A note on the fly-leaf shows that this transcript was owned in 1793 by Lieut.-Colonel Whitelocke, Lady Ouseley's father. *Now deposited in the Bodleian Library, Oxford.*

Ouseley MS 7 — Sir Gore Ouseley's Diary of his travels to Persia and Russia, 1810-15. *Now deposited in the Bodelain Library, Oxford.*

Ouseley MS 8 — Fly-leaves of Lady Ouseley's Bible containing entries made by Sir Gore and Sir Frederick Ouseley.

Ouseley MS 9 — Letter from Sir Gore Ouseley to the Prime Minister (Melbourne) asking permission for an additional heraldic supporter following his appointment to the Royal Guelphic Order, endorsed in another hand 'Extract of this letter referd. to Heralds' College, 10 Nov. 1831.'

Ouseley MS 10 — Four letters from Sir Henry Bishop to Sir Frederick Ouseley about his degrees in music, 1849-54.

B PRINTED

Abbreviation	
A&C	Alderson (M. F.) and Colles (H. C.), (editors), *History of St Michael's College Tenbury* (London, S.P.C.K 1943).
Bennett	Bennett (Frederick), *The Story of W. J. E. Bennett* (London, Longmans, Green and Co., 1909).
Havergal	Havergal (Francis Tebbs), *Memorials of Frederick Arthur Gore Ouseley* (London, Ellis & Elvey; Walsall, W. H. Robinson; Hereford, Jakeman and Carver, 1889).
Joyce	Joyce (Frederick Wayland), *The Life of Rev. Sir F. A. G. Ouseley, Bart.* (London, Methuen & Co., 1896). [F. W. Joyce was the grandson of James Joyce, Ouseley's tutor, and son of James Wayland Joyce, his lifelong intimate friend.]
Mem.	[Bumpus (John Skelton), (editor)], *Memorabilia. Fiftieth Anniversary 1906* (privately printed, 1907). [A record of the Jubilee Celebrations of St Michael's College.]
Reynolds	Reynolds (James), 'A Memoir of the late Right Hon. Sir Gore Ouseley, Bart.' prefixed to Ouseley (Gore), *Biographical Notices of Persian Poets* (London, Oriental Translation Fund, 1846).

Stainer — Stainer (John), 'The Character and Influence of the late Sir Frederick Ouseley', *Proceedings of the Musical Association*, vol. 16 (1889-90), pp. 25-39.

C MISCELLANEA

Box files of Programmes, Orders of Service, Prospectuses, photographs, and other ephemera relating to St Michael's College and its personalities.

CHAPTER END-NOTES

NOTES TO CHAPTER 1

1. See Ouseley MS 2 for these early family traditions.

2. For the genealogy from Richard to Ralph Ouseley and the biography of Gore Ouseley in general see Ouseley MS 1, much drawn on by Reynolds.

3. Reynolds, p.xxiii.

4. Joyce, pp 4-5.

5. Ouseley MS 5.

6. He appears to have regarded the Shah's grant as self-sufficient and did not seek permission for his use of these in England. Later, however, to preserve in his family a token of his appointment to the Order of Guelph, he wrote to the Prime Minister (Melbourne) in November 1831 to ask for royal authority to use the white horse of Guelph in this way. See Ouseley MS 9. The result is not known.

7. Ouseley MS 8. Gore Ouseley's personal diary of his Persian and Russian travels is Ouseley MS 7 from which Reynolds prints substantial extracts. The official documents relating to the diplomatic mission are in the British Library.

8. Havergal, p.7.

9. Sandys (W.) and Forster (S.A.), *History of the Violin* (London, 1864), p.206.

10. Ouseley MSS 1-4.

11. Joyce, p.4.

12. Ouseley MS 8.

NOTES TO CHAPTER 2

1. Ouseley MS 8.

2. Havergal, p.106; Joyce, p.12.

3. This portrait is said to have been exhibited at the Royal Academy in 1835. It was a familiar feature, first in the hall, then in the library, of St Michael's College, and is reproduced in both Joyce and A&C. Among others who sat for Lucas was the Duke of Wellington, Frederick Ouseley's godfather.

4. She wrote an account of his early skill, printed in Joyce, pp.17-25 and, with some fragmentary additions, in Havergal, pp.5-10. But though extant in 1889, her account was not with Ouseley's music when it was catalogued in the 1920s.

5. Bodleian Library, Oxford: Tenbury MSS 660, 759, 1087, 1087a, 1146, 1370-73, 1468a-b.

6. Quoted in Joyce, p.239 and Stainer, p.28.

7 *The Harmonicon*, vol.11 (1833), i, p.102.

8. Royal Archives: Princess Victoria's Journal. *Quoted by gracious permission of Her Majesty The Queen.*

9. Joyce, p.14.

10. *The Harmonicon*, loc.cit.

11. Joyce, p.26.

12. Mem., p.42.

13. Joyce, p.45.

14. *Oxford University Calendar, 1846.* Joyce's statement that he was awarded an 'honorary fourth' - whatever that may be - is an absurdity.

15. Joyce, p.48.

16. Ouseley MS 10.

17. For St Barnabas', Pimlico, see Bennett, Chapters IV-VII and pp.195-8, 205.

18. Joyce, p.52.

19. Ouseley's curacy under Bennett brought him into contact with the heart of this controversy, though not, of course, in any leading position. The vestry of St Paul's, Knightsbridge was the scene of a meeting on 9 March 1850 at which Manning presided and which resulted in a 'Declaration' printed in *The Times* on 20 March signed by Bennett, G. A. Denison, Keble, Manning, Pusey, J. G. Talbot, Robert and Henry Wilberforce and some others. See Gray (Robert), *Cardinal Manning* (1985) and Purcell (E. S.), *Life of Cardinal Manning* (2nd ed., 1896), vol.1.

20. Joyce, p.53.

21. Joyce, p.64.

22. Joyce, p.65.

23. Bennett, p.111.

24. Joyce, p.66.

25. Bennett, p.123. At the end of 1851 he became vicar of Frome, Somerset, whither Mary Jane and Alexandrine Ouseley went in order to work with him (ibid., p.210), and where they died in 1861 and 1862 respectively. (Ouseley MS 8).

26. These details are assembled from Bennett, loc. cit. & passim.

NOTES TO CHAPTER 3

1. Hampton MS.

2. Domus MS 1.

3. Hampton MS; Bennett, pp.268-9.

4. Joyce, Chapter IV, passim. All letters below dated 1851 are from this source.

5. Joyce, pp.81, 83.

6. A&C, p.14.

7. For Ouseley's early negotiations and problems generally at Tenbury, see Domus MS 2.

8. Calendered copy of the will, Public Record Office PROB 11/2159 (Section 723).

9. Joyce, p.83; A&C, p.16.

10. Domus MS 1.

11. Hampton MS.

12. Stainer, p.33.

13. Ouseley MS 10.

14. Joyce, p.85; unidentified newspaper cutting in J. S. Bumpus's extra-illustrated copy of Joyce.

15. Joyce, p.87.

16. A&C, pp.18-19.

17. Bodleian Library, Tenbury MS 1463A.

18. N&M MS 1.

19. Joyce, p.92; Bumpus, (J. S.), *A History of English Cathedral Music* (London, [1908]), vol.2, pp.562-3. Miss Rushout also presented the Communion plate.

20. N&M MS 2.

21. N&M MS 3.

22. Letter from Mr A. S. Miles dated 12 February 1903, in the archives of the National Society (C. of E.) for Promoting Religious Education. Log Book in the County of Hereford and Worcester Record Office.

23. A&C, p.26.

24. A&C, p.47.

25. Joyce, p.84. Unfortunately this has been accepted as authoritative by Nicholas Temperley in his important work *The Music of the English Parish Church* (Cambridge, C.U.P., 1979), vol.1, p.352.

NOTES TO CHAPTER 4

1. The sermon was published by Rivingtons, London, 1856.
2. Joyce, p.5, footnote.

3. For the events of 29 September 1856 generally see Joyce, pp.88-90. Details of the choir in Havergal, pp.64-5. Some personal recollections of the occasion by Bishop J.C.Corfe are in *St Michael's College Magazine* for December 1918. Here he says that the boys were temporarily accommodated at the Swan Hotel, Tenbury, not Spring Grove as stated in Chapter 3 above, relying on Joyce.

4. Miller's letter of 13 March 1857 and his private letter are printed in Joyce, pp.95-97. Ouseley's official reply was printed for subscribers. Copy in SMC Miscellanea. His private reply is with Domus MS 2. It is opportune to observe that John Miller (1787-1858) was no obscurantist but a man of a certain distinction. At Oxford he won the Chancellor's medal for Latin prose, became a Fellow of his College (Worcester) and earned the enduring, admiring friendship of Keble. After leaving Oxford for pastoral work he delivered the Bampton Lectures in 1817. Following two curacies and a living he settled in the family home at Bockleton in 1842 as assistant curate (for an absentee brother) of Leysters and Bockleton, becoming Vicar of Bockleton in 1855. At the time of Newman's deep perplexity in 1844 Keble suggested that he should consult Miller (which advice Newman did not take). There is a long and interesting obituary notice in *The Gentleman's Magazine*, 1858,i,pp.441-4. See also Coleridge (J.T.), *A Memoir of the Rev. John Keble*

(Oxford and London, J. Parker, 1869), pp.23-29; Lock (Walter), *John Keble* (London, Methuen 1893), pp.6-7; Battiscombe (Georgina), *John Keble. A Study in Limitations* (London, Constable, 1963), pp.249 and 284.

5. Domus MS 5(a).

6. Stainer, p.34.

7. Recollection of C.W.James in A&C, p.44.

8. Domus MS 5(a).

9. K.B.Macaulay in A&C, p.42.

10. G.C.E.Ryley in A&C, p.56.

11. A few printed programmes for the Commemoration festival and its associated secular concert are in SMC Miscellanea.

12. Details of admissions, parentage, and subsequent careers of boys are derived from Domus MS 4(a), maintained in an unidentified hand in Ouseley's day.

13. Letter belonging to the late Sir John Dykes Bower, to whom I owe sight of this and other letters.

14. A&C, p.44.

15. Details from Domus MS 3.

16. Another copy in SMC Miscellanea.

17. *St Michael's College Magazine*, July 1959. Lahee was the son of the composer of the well-known hymn tune *Nativity*. How these reminiscences reached the *Magazine* does not appear. Presumably they were printed posthumously.

18. Stainer, p.34.

19. Hampton MS.

20. Programme for 1883 in SMC Miscellanea.

21. I owe this reference to Professor Nicholas Temperley.

22. Church Congress Reports of Proceedings, 1874, pp.96-101.

23. Joyce, p.160.

24. Havergal. p.39.

25. Joyce, p.107.

26. Joyce, p.109. A small group of Ouseley's letters to M.F.Alderson is Domus MS 8.

27. A sentence wisely omitted by the editors of A&C from the reminiscences of K.B.Macaulay, pp.40-42. The original is with SMC Miscellanea.

28. A&C, p.46.

29. A list of subscribers with other information is with SMC Miscellanea.

30. Report of funeral in the *Tenbury Advertiser*, printed in Havergal, p.12.

31. Obituary notices printed *in extenso* in Havergal, pp.11-35.

32. Fellows' minutes.

33. For these biographical details and his financial relations with the College see Hampton MS.

34. Communicated by Elgar to Sir Percy Hull who told the present writer.

35. A printed pamphlet relating to its first 16 years is in SMC Miscellanea.

36. 'A visit to Sir Frederick Ouseley's "study"', *Monthly Music Record*, vol.26 (1896), pp.223-4; 'A visit to Tenbury', *The Musical Times*, vol.41 (1900), pp.713-19.

37. For details and the texts of sermons see Mem.

NOTES TO CHAPTER 5

1. Ouseley was ready togive a hearing to music by friends or protégés, for example A.H.D.Prendergast, Richard Mann (a lay clerk), William Claxton (former chorister, later organist), or the Earl of Mar (formerly an adult commoner).

2. Letter belonging to the late Sir John Dykes Bower.

3. Letter belonging to the late Sir John Dykes Bower.

4. Domus MS 5(a-c).

5. Bodleian Library: Tenbury MS 1033.

6. Though irrelevant, one cannot forbear a comment on this curious series. Published expressly as 'suited for Parochial use' and therefore in handy leaflet form, yet it employed C clefs and included such things as *Why art thou so heavy, O my soul* (Gibbons), *When the Son of Man* (Locke) with its long bass solo, Tomkins's *Great and marvellous*, and Blow's elaborately disposed *Praise the Lord, O my soul*. It cannot be said that Cope set his sights low.

NOTES TO CHAPTER 6

1. *The Times* obituary notice, 15 November 1948.

2. A&C, p.60.

3. Information about Gould's books from E.H.Fellowes. With regard to art treasures possessed by Ouseley it has been stated (A&C, p.80) that 'the mystery of the disappearance of his priceless Cellini vase, for example, has never been solved.' The present author has been unable to discover any ground for believing that Ouseley possessed such a vase, and must beg leave to doubt it. Among Gore Ouseley's books there survives a copy of the sale catalogue of the contents of Strawberry Hill collected by Horace Walpole (auctioned by George Robins, 25 April 1842 and following days) in which there is a rough pencil mark, *'vide'*, against a lot described on p.157 as 'The renowned silver bell, made expressly for Pope Clement VII by ... Benvenuto Cellini': but that is not a vase and such a mark is no evidence that Sir Gore acquired it.

4. A&C, p.71.

5. Domus MS 5(f-h).

6. The account of Fellowes's appointment and his work as Librarian is from personal knowledge.

7. The bulk of information in this chapter for which no specific reference is given is taken from the Minute Book of the Governing Body and *St Michael's College Magazine* of relevant date. Swann initiated this periodical in 1918.

NOTES TO CHAPTER 7

1. For Buckmaster's own account see A&C, pp.64-66.

2. For Billen's own account of war-time at St Michael's College see A&C, pp.67-69. Recollections of him and his regime by an Old Boy of the period may be found in the *St Michael's College Magazine*, 1955.

3. Domus MS 5(h-j).

4. On his death there was an obituary notice in *The Times*, 5 June 1961.

5. Messrs Sotheby's Sale Catalogue, 22-23 October 1956.

NOTE TO CHAPTER 8

1. Messrs Sotheby's Sale Catalogue, 26 June 1978 with detailed foreword by the present editor. The Collection was bought complete by Pierre Berès, a Parisian dealer, and most of the volumes have gone to fill gaps in kindred collections in the Bibliothèque nationale in Paris or the Bibliothèque de Versailles.

NOTES TO CHAPTER 10

1. The source of this information is unknown. - Editor.

2. An extensive account of Tenbury MSS 346-7 may be found in *A Textual and Historical Companion to Handel's 'Messiah'* by the present editor (London, Novello and Co., 1965).

3. On the outside cover is a majuscule 'E', the prominent serifs of which led Fellowes to the mistaken conclusion that it was a monogram 'TE', causing him to suggest that it may have actually belonged to Thomas East. But such a letter was customarily used to identify the set of books to which a given part belonged.

4. For a precisely documented account of the provenance of the Toulouse-Philidor Collection, with details of the investigations carried out by Fellowes, see the present editor's Foreword to Sotheby's Sale Catalogue, 26 June 1978.

This edition consists of 450 copies